Kursaal Memories

Kursaal Memories

A History of Southend's Amusement Park

KEN CROWE

SKELTER
PUBLISHING

First published in 2003 by
Skelter Publishing LLP
3 Connaught Road
St Albans
Herts
AL3 5RX

A catalogue record for this book is available
From the British Library

ISBN 0 9544573 0 7

This book was designed by:
Skelter Publishing LLP

Designed and Typeset in Great Britain by Paul Barrett Book Production

Printed by Antony Rowe Ltd, Chippenham, Wiltshire

Contents

CHAPTER ONE

In the Beginning 1

    Early fairgrounds and the Marine Park 2

CHAPTER TWO

Grand openings and big crowds 8

    The Kursaal 9
    The Luna Park 14

CHAPTER THREE

The first C.J. Morehouse 16

    Forward with an enterprising man 17
    Rifles, the Rink and Marie Lloyd 17
    Gypsies, soldiers and the zoo 19

CHAPTER FOUR

The David de Forest Morehouse years (1921–1934) 23

    The Spurs are united 24
    The Water Chute and the railway that never stopped 24
    Fully booked for winter 28
    Slots of fun 29
    Zulus, artificial ice and Sacco, the fasting man 29
    Motorbikes, midgets and Eric the Whale 32
    Bostock's Wonder Zoo 35
    Noah's Ark, Mont Blanc and Al Capone's Car 36
    'One Bright Spot' 38
    Kursaal characters of the inter-war years 38

CHAPTER FIVE

The Kursaal under Trustees 1935 to 1947 46

    In safe hands 47
    The Cyclone 47
    The Tornado 49
    Another war, the ballroom and plans for the zoo 50
    Lights out for the cinema 51
    Uniforms, waterproofs and the NAAFI 51
    Restored and repaired 55
    The stars come out 56

CHAPTER SIX

C.J. Morehouse (the second) 1948–1973 57

    The Kursaal in its heyday 58
    Bands and bandleaders 64
    Fanny Craddock, bungalows and the circus 72
    A lady hits the wall 82

CHAPTER SEVEN

An era ends, another begins 1973–1998 96

    Goodbye to all that 97
    Closure and re-development 101
    Hello to all this! 104

Select Bibliography 107

Footnotes 108

Preface

It is always pleasing to see any aspect of the English seaside taken on by a good historian. Its buildings and pleasure gardens are generally under-researched and are rarely accorded the respect they deserve, being by definition provincial and often ephemeral, although the latter is far from the case for Southend's Kursaal. Ken Crowe has provided us with an admirable history of this pleasure dome, from its origins as a putative rival to Blackpool Tower, through its shaky early days, into its interwar and 1950s heydays, and finally to its remodelling and reopening. His painstaking account of the huge variety of entertainments available – a tribute to the inventiveness of the English seaside entrepreneur – throws light on the social history of the times, and includes such unforgettable acts as Eric the Whale, bowls-playing dolphins and a complete Balkan Village, as well as an appearance from a personal favourite, the band Manfred Mann. Women have always played a large part in the Kursaal story, from the mysterious Monday Ladies of the thirties, who came down in their droves from the East End to have a good time, to the entertainments aimed at housewives of the fifties; 1955 was an especially good year, with the Happy Housewives exhibition and Fanny Craddock making Kitchen Magic. If all human life was not already at the Kursaal, then it would probably be in one of next week's acts. It is a pleasure to read such a well-researched book on a seaside attraction which has come to life again; Ken Crowe's story has a happy ending.

Lynn F. Pearson
Architectural Historian
January 2003

Acknowledgements

It would have been impossible to compile a book such as this without the help of a very large number of people, particularly those people who have first hand memories of the Kursaal. The author wishes to thank Chris Izod for his constant help and advice, Alan Stack, Chairman of the Rowallan Group and Roy Peck, Technical Director of the Rowallan Group for their help. A great deal of help has been given and photographs lent, by people who worked at the Kursaal, or who appeared in pop concerts, and other musical events, or who were regular visitors to the fairground and buildings, including Clive Rawlins, Mrs Yvonne Chapman, Barry Lecorgne, Mrs Nunn, Ray Catling of the Ray King Trio, Bob Charman of the Spectres, Ron Pankhurst of the Del Rio Five, Mrs Jean White, Mrs Theresa Dipper, Mrs June Lemaire, Mrs A. King, Joe Stumcke, Mr L. Pitt, Dennis Hayward, Alf Saunders, Chris Woodward, Mrs E. Beebee, Mr Humphreys, John Coppings, Joe Strothard, Les Bass and Howard Lead from The Barronets, Frank Cornish of Frankie and the Dreamweavers, Richard Abrey, Laurie Gimbrett, Doreen Sparrow, Ken Westell, Gary Edwards, Jackie Johnston and David Oxley. I would also like to thank Bob Bradley of Margate Local History Museum for information regarding the Margate Kursaal scheme, Dr Vanessa Toulmin and her colleagues at the National Fairground Archive, Mrs Sue Gough Local Studies Librarian at Southend Library and the staff of the Southend branch of the Essex Record Office for their patient help and advice. A special debt of thanks is due to my colleague David Mitchell of the Southend Museums Service for converting the typescript and photographs into a form ready for printing.

Introduction

One Bright Spot and **By the Dome it's Known** were bywords for the Kursaal, certainly in Southend, in the East End of London and throughout much of southern England. The Kursaal was the largest amusement park in the south throughout much of the twentieth century and the destination for thousands of East Enders and others up to the 1960s. This book tells the story of the Kursaal: from its origins in the late nineteenth century, to the closure of the park and gardens in the 1970s, and the closure of the buildings in the 1980s, and then finally to the high profile re-opening of the 'new' Kursaal in 1998.

What does the word Kursaal mean? According to Hutchinson's *Dictionary of Difficult Words*, the term refers to an entertainment hall, public room or hotel at a spa or seaside resort. The word is German in origin, and there are certainly *Kursaals* on the Continent. There they are cure-halls – public rooms in spas where the sick go to recuperate or recover. The word seems to have been adapted in this country to mean a place of entertainment, perhaps healthy entertainment, at a seaside resort. That the word Kursaal has come to be associated with a place of entertainment, a 'pleasure palace' is illustrated by its use in fiction; for example, being used in the title of a Dr. Who book of 1998, in which The Doctor and Sam travel to a planet being made into a giant pleasure palace, a Kursaal.

In order to place the building of the Southend Kursaal in its historic context, it is important to mention the, often unfulfilled, attempts to build such pleasure palaces in the later nineteenth and earlier twentieth centuries. Attempts to lure the visitor from the nearest large urban centres resulted in a multitude of resort-based entertainment companies, each financed by share ownership, the shareholders often being local businessmen, sometimes entrepreneurs, and sometimes very large concerns with local connections. These limited liability companies planned to build such attractions as winter gardens, piers, towers and Kursaals, but many were unsuccessful. Rarely could enough capital be raised to complete the ambitious projects of their founders and, as we shall see, one company frequently gave rise to another, in attempts to carry on the schemes.

There was a short-lived Kursaal at Bexhill-on-Sea. Built by the Eighth Earl De La Warr, it was part of his plan to develop Bexhill into a fashionable seaside resort. This Kursaal, established by the Bexhill Kursaal and Winter Gardens Ltd (of 1899), was a pavilion or theatre, and did not house sideshows or amusement machines. There were plans to build a Kursaal at Margate, but these never got off the drawing board. In 1908 the Isle of Wight Kursaals and Entertainments Company was established, and in 1913 the Hove Pier, Theatre and Kursaal Company was formed, but neither of these Kursaals was ever built[1].

Southend was the nearest seaside resort to London. Following Sir John Lubbock's Bank Holiday Act of 1871, the first Monday in August became a national holiday, and the London, Tilbury and Southend Railway Company posted bills on hoardings all over London advertising Southend as the capital's nearest resort. In 1883 the *East London Observer* commented:

Everyone seemed to recognise that the August Holiday was, of all others, the one for suburban outings or seaside trips rather than the peculiar enjoyments derivable from parading the streets.

On Wanstead Heath the East Ender could enjoy the toy stalls, photographic studios, coconut shies, kiss-in-the-ring, pony and donkey riding, steam roundabouts and swings. Some resorts, Eastbourne and Bournemouth, for example, excluded such amusements, but at Southend such entertainment had been provided, seasonally, for many years on the seafront greens. Southend became known as Whitechapel-on-Sea. When the Marine Park, and then the Kursaal opened, they provided the same sort of entertainments, but this time, bigger and better.

The Kursaal remained a major destination, especially for day-trippers and works outings from the East End of London, until the 1960s. There were several annual events for which the Kursaal was justly famous. These included the New Year's Eve Ball, the charity dinner for deprived children, sponsored by the Alexandra Yacht Club, and the Old People's Dinner. The Kursaal was used as the setting for scenes in a number of films and episodes of television shows, among them *The Avengers, The Prisoner, Nearest and Dearest* (when it was supposed to be Blackpool!) and the films *Over the Moon* and *Twenty-One Days*[2]. The Kursaal was largely self-supporting, with its own ice-cream and rock factories, greenhouses and laundry. A combination of factors resulted in declining visitor numbers especially from the mid-1960s onwards. Cheap package holidays to the sun, and the growth of sight-seeing tours took a large number of visitors to the Mediterranean or to the West Country, especially following the advent of paid holidays and increased motor car ownership. Southend, like many other large towns, looked towards changing its image in the 1960s, modernising the town centre and seeking a new economic base. Added to that, in the 1960s and 1970s many new entertainment centres were opening in Southend, including the Cliffs Pavilion. Times were changing, but the Kursaal was not changing with them. The closing song *There's No Business Like Show Business* was played over the tannoy for the last time in the early 1970s.

As the reader will discover, as with many fairs and fairgrounds, the Kursaal was very much a family institution. Generations of the same family worked at the park, as concessionaires (tenants) or employees, and in some cases for as long as the Kursaal existed.

The purpose of this book is to trace in some detail the history of Southend's Kursaal. It is not the intention here, and it would be impossible, to include people's own memories or accounts of their experiences, except where they relate to specific points in the narrative. Everybody who visited the Kursaal will have their own memories, and their own story to tell. Here we wish to give in outline the main facts and, hopefully, for those who remember the Kursaal, to stimulate those memories. For those wanting to hear and see more of people's memories, we can do no better than to recommend the video and audio tapes on the Kursaal, details of which are in the bibliography at the end of this book.

The principal sources used in the compilation of this book comprise the Kursaal Archive, mainly photographic, which was deposited with Southend Museums Service by the Kursaal Estates Ltd following the closure of the Kursaal in 1986; articles and advertisements in the local press together with a very brief and unpublished history of the Kursaal compiled by the Kursaal Estates Ltd. Other sources have included original records in the Public Record Office and Essex Record Office and cuttings books from various sources. Transcripts from taped interviews with Kursaal employees and others have provided very useful background information, as have more recent interviews with past Kursaal workers.

One

In the Beginning

The Pier Hill Fairground was established by 1889. It featured swings, steam roundabouts and the "Roly-Poly" ride, passengers in which, we are told, could experience all the joys of complete seasickness without the danger of leaving dry land! Reproduced courtesy of Essex Records Office (ERO D/DS 229/22).

Early fairgrounds and the Marine Park

The first areas to be used as fairgrounds or for amusements in Southend were the 'greens' which stretched along the seafront, on the beach side of what became Marine Parade. The greens had been used for cricket games in the summer, and were the temporary location of fun fairs in the nineteenth century. One of the greens, known from the later nineteenth century as Pawley's Green, appears to have been the site of the first fairly permanent (although no doubt seasonal) fair ground in the town. The green was named after John Pawley, who took over the green or *The Park* as it was also known, in 1869[3]. In 1885 a letter of complaint appeared in the *Southend Standard*, regarding the noise from a new shooting gallery on Pawley's Green; the letter had been written by a Mr Collingwood Wilson, who claimed to have occupied an adjacent green for 26 years and used *'the old and safe rifles … and have never had a complaint.'*

In 1887 the Southend Local Board considered the purchase of Pawley's Green, and the removal of all the amusements[4]. In his column in the *Southend Standard*, 'Rambler' commented that he was

> *rather dubious as to the wisdom of the apparent intention of sweeping away all the unorthodox amusements and noises. There must be some place in Southend where certain classes of excursionists may enjoy themselves in their own way and unless the householders very near very strongly object to what goes on on Pawley's Green it will be mischievous to interfere very seriously.*

The Green was not purchased at that time, and the complaints, now regarding a hirdy-girdy and steam roundabout, continued. The Green was eventually purchased by the Council in 1900[5].

In January 1888 Southend Local Board had received an application from the Gravity Switchback Railway Company for the erection of one of their rides in Southend. The Local Board suggested a site in front of Strutt's Parade, a section of Marine Parade, resulting in a barrage of objections[6]. The following year plans were submitted for a switchback railway and shooting gallery to be built on Pier Hill[7]. This was the origin of the Pier Hill Fairground, which opened in June 1889.

The following excerpt from an article in the *Southend Standard* in 1893 gives an impression of the sorts of amusements that were provided on an August Bank Holiday in Southend at this time:

> *In this part of the town the crowds were decidedly considerable and surging for the most part towards the fair paraphernalia. Here were the weighing machines, fortune tellers, shooting galleries, swings and coconut shies, and all appeared to be patronised with liberality…To many it was the only holiday away from home which they would get during the year, and consequently while they were out for a day of pleasure, they banished all care and trouble.*

In 1871 the Bank Holidays Act, promoted by Sir John Lubbock, had been passed, allowing bank workers and others (such as factory workers) an extra day's holiday on the first Monday in August. When the second railway line to Southend opened in 1889, competition between the rail companies kept fares at a level which could be afforded by all but the very poorest of the East Enders, whose seasonal patronage was so important to the railway at this time.

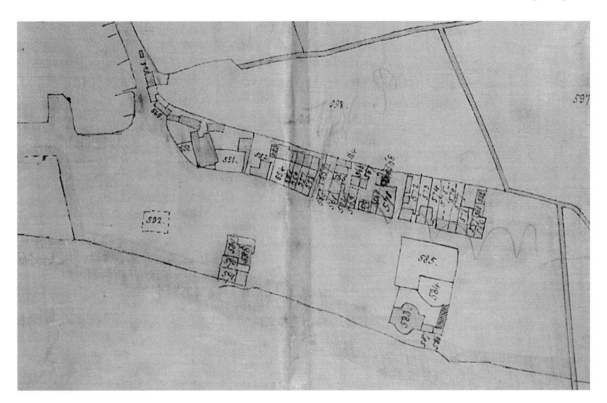

There were many letters published in the local newspapers from people complaining of the unruly behaviour of the trippers. Thomas Arnold, the tenant of Thames Farm (which partly occupied the site of the later Marine Park), who suffered at the hands of the trippers, complained that Southend had become the playground for the 'lower classes of excursionists'. Another correspondent explained the reason for the influx of trippers every August: 'This is the only seaside resort that the very poorest of our London factory hands and match box girls can be brought to and taken home again for 1/6d.'

In 1893 the father and son partnership of Alfred and Bernard Wiltshire Tolhurst, solicitors, expressed their intention of building a park in the eastern part of the town, for the benefit of visitors. They proposed to purchase about 15 acres of the Beaumont Building Estate, on the corner of Marine Parade and Brewery Road for the park, and employed H.E. Milner, a well-known landscape gardener and author of *Art and Practice of Landscape Gardening*[8], to carry out the scheme. Details of the proposals were given in the *Southend Observer*. The park would include a fresh water lake, fed from springs rising at the back of Mr Arnold's farm, which was intended for boating in the summer and skating in the winter. There would be an area for cricket and football, a running or bicycle track around the sports ground; a bandstand was also to be provided together with tennis courts and bowling green.

At the beginning of 1894 a further four acres had been added to the park as the Marine Park Recreational Annexe, and the Mayor of Southend, Alderman Gossett, was invited to open the park on 1 August of that year. However, the Mayor was forced to decline the offer, owing to very poor health, and the Marine Park was opened without ceremony. Apart from the lengthy walks, gardens and other garden features, there was a full programme of entertainment and amusements. These included Mademoiselle de Rosa's lady dancers, Lieutenant Taylor with

Thames Farm, the last tenant of which was Thomas Arnold, was sold for development at the end of the 19th Century. The southern part of this land (shown here) was incorporated into the Marine Park, later to become the Kursaal Gardens.

The Tolhursts commissioned the well-known landscape gardener, H. E. Milner, to design the Marine Park gardens. The main features were the walks and shrubberies, lake, bandstand and trotting track.

An early postcard view of the Marine Park, probably dating to around 1900. Notice in the background the newly built houses in Woodgrange Drive. This road had been built on the site of the original lane leading to Thames Farm.

his performing dogs, and J.B. Johnson and his niece, Ada, who performed aquatic tricks such as eating, drinking and smoking under water. The amusements or rides included a switchback railway, a dancing platform, swings and round-abouts, an aerial flight and several others were soon to be added, including a shooting gallery, *Shooting Jungle* and illusion show[9].

Early in 1896 Alfred Tolhurst leased part of the park to the Pyramidical Railway Company, who had recently purchased the patent of a new ride of that name. The Company was a successor to the Syndicate of the same name, the principal shareholders of which were Sir Augustus Harris, Annie Pitt, and Richard John Gifford Read of Westminster, consultant engineer for the Blackpool Tower scheme[10]. The Company had a nominal capital of £85,000, in one pound shares. It was announced in the local press that the Company intended to spend about £20,000 on building a Pyramidical Railway ride and a Cowdrey's patent Switchback steeplechase. In December 1896 the Company deposited with Southend Council a plan (no. 1359) for the erection of a tower and buildings at the south west corner of the park, adjacent to Southchurch Avenue. The architect of the buildings was to be George Sherrin, and the engineer was Mr R.J. Gifford Read[11].

A large coloured drawing of the proposed buildings was prepared. The parallels with the Blackpool Pleasure Beach and Tower are not hard to find, particularly since Gifford Read was the consultant engineer for the Tower. The main features of the Southend scheme were the red brick facade along Southchurch Avenue, a series of domes (the largest over the corner entrance), and a four hundred foot tower, at the top of which were to be stalls for the selling of souvenirs. A concert or Assembly Hall would accommodate 5,000 people, while to the left

Alfred Tolhurst who, together with his son, Bernard Wiltshire Tolhurst, bought up the land for the creation of the Marine Park, in the early 1890s.

Before the Kursaal buildings were erected, on their site stood a group of shops and houses, including Child's Ice Cream shop. This photograph was taken probably about 1895.

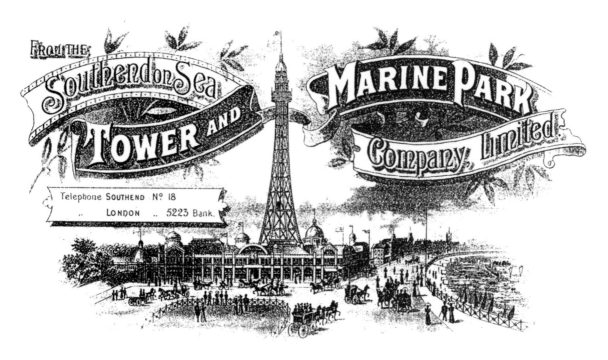

of the entrance was the dining or refreshment hall. There was also to be an Aviary House, leading to the zoological department, and the entrance to the Marine Park.

The designs were altered later, with the inclusion of a long arcade leading to a large octagon with sideshows. The Tower was now to have three observation platforms, and between its legs a hippodrome and water tanks for aquatic displays. By now a new company had been formed to carry out the scheme, the Southend-on-Sea Tower and Marine Park Company Limited, incorporated in December 1897[12]. This new company adopted the drawing of the proposed buildings as their letterhead. Their intention was 'To erect at Southend ... a Palace or Pavilion and other buildings including a Tower.'[13] By this date, 1898, Sherrin was working on the design with John Clarke[14]. However, despite all the grand designs and promises, the Pyrammidical Syndicate went into liquidation in February 1899, followed closely by the Company of the same name.

Revised plans for the buildings had been deposited in January 1899[15]. In August 1899 the Southend-on-Sea Tower and Marine Park Company Limited was renamed the Margate and Southend Kursaals Limited. This had a nominal share capital of £175,000. The shareholders included John Hall, gent, of Westcliff, Alfred Henry John Talbot White, auctioneer of Southend, and the Marine Palace Company Limited (Margate), but one of the largest shareholders in this new Company was Samuel Allsopp and Sons, brewers. The Kursaals Company (as it was often called) retained the services of George Sherrin and Gifford Read. The Pyramidical Syndicate had planned to take over the site of the Marine Palace at Margate (which had been destroyed in a storm in 1897), for the erection of a new building, with a domed entrance, and with dining and dancing halls, billiard saloon, etc[16]. The Kursaals Company, as inheritors of the plans of the Syndicate, were to build Kursaals at both towns (hence the name of the new company), the Margate Kursaal to be run in connection with the Southend one. It was also suggested that a line of pleasure steamers should ply between the two towns. However, the Margate site was left uncompleted, and it was not until 1905 that we find work commencing again at Margate, Sir Hiram Maxim being the chief promoter, and Allsopp recorded as a chief investor. The Margate Kursaal, however, was never completed[17].

The plans for the Southend Kursaal were passed, and building commenced. Meanwhile the attractions in the park included athletics meetings, dancing on the platform, switchback rides and swings. By the spring of 1901 the buildings were nearly complete. The grand entrance was surmounted by the 'spacious dome, through which the light of heaven filters with delightful effect.' The dance hall (and theatre) had a floor in polished oak parquet laid on 8040 springs by Goodall, Heighway and Lamb of Manchester, at a cost of £3,000. (The same firm had been retained for the laying of the ballroom floor at the ill-fated Margate Kursaal.) The 120-foot long arcade had shops to either side, leading to the hippodrome or circus. In May 1901 the concrete foundations of the 530-foot tower could be seen. The tower, of course, was never built.

Two

Grand openings and big crowds

The Kursaal from the south, taken in 1901, before the "improvement" of Marine Parade. To the right is the Warwick Revolving Tower, in the Britannia Fun Fair.

The Kursaal

The Kursaal was opened on 24 July 1901 by Lord Claud Hamilton, chairman of the Great Eastern Railway Company. The terrible weather did not deter a large crowd from witnessing the ceremony. In attendance were the Mayor, Town Clerk and Aldermen of the Borough, Lieutenant Colonel Tufnell, the member of Parliament, and R.A. Jones, among many other distinguished guests. The Kursaal, it was declared at the opening, would provide a great and permanent source of enjoyment to the toiling masses of the City of London.

The Kursaals Company, however, was now obviously in financial difficulties and Edward Cecil Moore was appointed Receiver. In February 1900 the chief shareholders, Samuel Allsopp and Sons, had mortgaged their leasehold property (the Kursaal and Marine Park) to Alfred Tolhurst. Subsequently they broke the terms of their deed of mortgage by dismantling the Pyramidal ride, thus forfeiting to Tolhurst the full mortgage price of £80,000. In 1902 the Margate and Southend Kursaals Limited was dissolved but despite all of these financial difficulties, the Kursaal remained open, with Mr George Scott as manager. Attractions included the Monster Phonograph of Mr Eddison in the Circus, and Grand Variety Entertainment in

THE ARCADE. — THE CIRCUS.

THE BALL ROOM.

The interior of the buildings, from an early advertising brochure. The Arcade was laid out to simulate a street in Cairo, and to the left of the entrance was the Café Chantant, later to become the Cinema.

the Ballroom, and the Kursaal was soon advertised as 'The most popular place of Entertainment on the South Coast'. In the central arcade, decorated to represent a street in Cairo, were shooting galleries, electric fishponds, 'art museums', and 'the latest Yankee notions'. In September 1903 the Wild West came to the Kursaal in the person of Buffalo Bill (W.E. Cody) with his troupe of horse riders. However, that year the buildings closed early for the season, and the Marine Park and Kursaal were put up for sale by auction. The Kursaal

The trotting track was completed in 1905, and was one of the earliest attractions, together with the switchback railway, aerial flight, dancing platform and "swanneries."

The trotting track was the major feature in the Marine Park. Originally laid out for the popular sport of "trotting", the centre of the track was used for open-air sports, including cricket matches and competitions between fire crews.

The Aerial Flight was among the earliest attractions in the Park, dating from 1894. It was also one of the longest surviving of the early rides, being a feature into the 1930s.

Arsene Lecorgne, seen here with his son, was one of the first showmen to occupy a place in the Marine Park. Coming over from northern France in 1901, he set up a number of sideshows in the park, including the Dandies, Hoopla and coconut shies.

was described as the Renowned Marine Park and Popular Pleasure Palace of the favourite Health Resort, with grand Concert Hall, Theatre or Ball Room, Tea Balcony, Magnificent Dining Hall, Billiard Saloon for Four Tables, Eight Refreshment Bars, 2 Arcades of 37 shops, Hippodrome and Menagerie, and Dome of noble proportions. Despite the best efforts of the authors of the Sale Particulars, the sale attracted no buyers and Allsopps remained the reluctant owners, much to the annoyance of the Company's shareholders, one of whom blamed the declining fortunes of the company on 'that wildcat scheme'.

The Kursaal re-opened for the new season on 23 May 1904 and was billed as 'the People's Palace – the best Amusement Resort in or out of London'. The Kursaal Cycle and Athletic Club and the Southend Cycling Club continued to meet in the Marine Park, and by the end of 1905 the Trotting Track had been completed. In the centre of the track took place football and

Another of the early tenants of the grounds was Fred Houchin. Like the Lecorgnes, generations of the Houchin family maintained their connection with the Kursaal until the closure of the park.

Mr. Houchin (Jolly Tubes)

Mr. J.K. Sykes (Menagerie)

Mr. Wilford (Grounds Manager)

Mr. T. Wales (Aerial Flight)

Mr. Crouch (Zoo)

The Arcade was always the home for the main side shows, such as rifle ranges and hoopla stands. The owners of the stands would encourage passers by to "have a go" often giving away the first few prizes to encourage others to join in.

athletic meetings, open-air boxing matches, and displays by competing fire brigades. Introduced at this time were a number of shows and exhibitions that were to become a regular feature of the Kursaal in later years. Among these were beauty shows, mother and baby shows, wrestling matches (including the famous 'Terrible Turk' Madrali and Takka – a Japanese jujitsu champion – in 1906), an Industrial Exhibition and the Kursaal Band competition. In 1907, 25 July was declared *Daily Mirror Day*; the newspaper offering its readers tickets on special excursion trains from London at half the normal fare, with free entry to the Kursaal.

Descriptions of the Kursaal in these early days mention a bandstand that used to be under the dome (probably seasonally) and the Arcade, which was lined with booths, rifle ranges and hoop-la stands. There was also a quick-sketch artist ready to draw any passing customer. Leading from the Dome there was the large Café Chantant, where artists appearing in Music Hall at the time used to entertain the patrons between the shows. In 1907, for example, Mr George Menva entertained the patrons with 'his wonderful Indian and Egyptian feats' and at the far end of the Arcade was the circus ring, and the Kursaal menagerie. Two of the earliest concessionaires were Arsene Jules Lecorgne and Fred Houchin who brought with them a variety of sideshows and amusements, which are described later.

The Luna Park

Two further attempts were made to sell the Kursaal, but in 1910 the *Southend and Westcliff Graphic* reported that negotiations were nearing completion between Allsopps and the Luna Park and Palace of Amusements, Southend-on-Sea. The Luna Park Company had been registered in 1910 by its founder, Thomas William Hilton, of Rochdale, with the specific intention of acquiring the buildings and land and to carry on and extend the business. The attractions to be installed by the new owners were an aero flight, the River Caves and two wooden roller coasters: the Harton Scenic Railway, measuring 1700 feet in length, and the Figure of Eight coaster. The Harton Scenic Railway was named after the Harton Company in Pittsburgh, which designed and built the ride. A winter garden was to be installed in the entrance and the ballroom was to be converted into a 'place of entertainment of the Vaudeville type'. It was also planned to introduce an American bowling alley. The new general manager, Mr J. White, was reported as saying that 'Southend was on the eve of one of the greatest booms in entertainment this country had ever known'. The Luna Park and Palace opened for the season on Saturday 18 June 1910 and one of the first attractions for visitors was the airship *America*, which was to attempt a transatlantic crossing. The *Southend and Westcliff Graphic* reported:

A general view of the Kursaal grounds taken about 1910. One of the principal attractions at this time was the Joy Wheel, introduced by the new owners, the Luna Park Company.

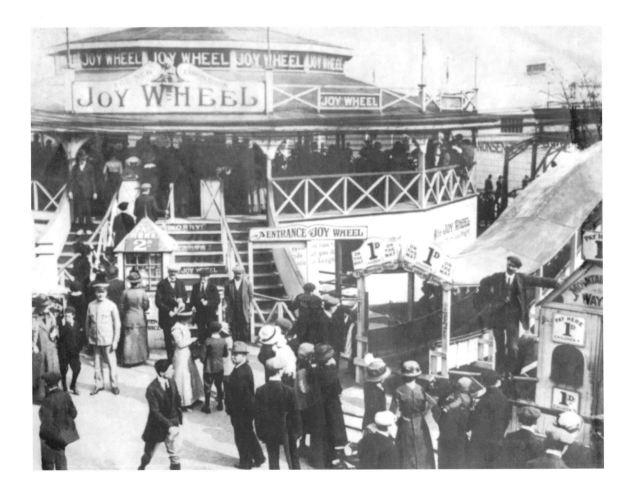

To see the crowds waiting for the cars on the scenic railway or the numbers outside the 'figure-of-eight' reminds one of the Anglo-Jap Exhibition, whilst the multiplicity of attractions is hardly paralleled in the Metropolis itself. Novelties have been brought from the Continent. The Joy Wheel, a delightful mechanical amusement was one of the principal attractions at the Brussels Exhibition. The American Bowling Alley brings its own welcome. The Mysterious Caves cause laughter from morning till night, Astley's Circus is first class, while Distorting Mirrors are a continuous source of amusement.

A view of the Kursaal about 1910.

There was also a miniature railway, said to be one of the new wonders of the world, together with a real aeroplane. The Luna Park was advertised as the 'White City of Southend', the miniature railway now running right around the grounds, and said to be the longest in England. In June 1911 the Joy Wheel was destroyed by fire, but was soon replaced by the new Joy Wheel[18].

It was claimed that over the Easter holiday of 1911 over 100,000 people had patronised the park and buildings. But only about half the park was laid out for amusements and Bram Stevens, who visited and worked in the Kursaal from the earliest days, remembered the weed-infested wilderness that covered much of the area. Despite the numbers of visitors, the Luna Park was not the financial success hoped for, and in 1912 was sold and the Luna Park Company went into liquidation.

THREE

The first C.J. Morehouse

Clifton Jay Morehouse purchased the Luna Park in 1912, changing its name immediately back to Kursaal. He also immediately formed the first Southend (Kursaal) Scout group.

Forward with an enterprising man

The new owner was Clifton Jay Morehouse and he had purchased the enterprise outright. A businessman and industrialist who had invented the gas radiator in America, and later moved to Birmingham in England, Morehouse stated his intention to build houses on half the grounds, reserving two areas for cricket and football. The area reserved for amusements was to be called the Kursaal Gardens. C.J. Morehouse was to be Managing Director and his son, David de Forest Morehouse, general manager. Advertising was essential to the success of the Kursaal and, in addition to posters at the Kursaal entrance and at railway stations, Mr. Morehouse employed several men to walk the town with portmanteaux bearing the message 'I am also looking for the Kursaal. See you there tonight'. C.J. Morehouse also formed the First Southend (Kursaal) Scouts in the same year.

Rifles, the Rink and Marie Lloyd

John Backhouse was appointed manager of the Kursaal Picture Theatre, and among the first films to be shown under his management were *The Spanish Cavalier*, *The Vengeance of Mafia*, and *Counsel for the Defence*. The cinema originally operating in the ballroom, with Ruffles Imperial Bioscope, opened weekdays from 6.00pm until 10.30pm and on Saturdays there were children's matinees, from 2.30pm until 5.20pm. Following the Cinematograph Act of 1909 the original Café Chantant was converted to cinema use as the Kursaal Kinema.

In 1913 a school of golf was opened in the Kursaal (lessons three shillings per hour, or a course of six lessons for 15 shillings), together with indoor bowls and cricket practice. The

Another early feature of Morehouse's Kursaal was the Kursaal Rifle Club. During the First World War the rifle range was used for practice by the regiments who were stationed there.

Among the many side shows and stalls that were such a feature of the Marine Park and Kursaal was the Pot-Em stall, seen here probably shortly before the First World War.

Another main attraction in the Kursaal grounds during the First World War was the replica of the British trenches at Ypres. The Kursaal remained open throughout the period of the war.

Circus was converted to a dancing and skating hall, with a floor of pitch pine; this became known as the Crystal Rink. At the end of the year the Ideal Home and Industrial Exhibition was held at the Kursaal, with nearly four acres of exhibits, and in February the following year, the Exhibition of Industries, including the 'Electric Home' based on the original at the Ideal Home Exhibition, Olympia.

Marie Lloyd appeared at the Kursaal in January 1914, a year that also saw the introduction of several new amusements, including the House of Nonsense, an early fun house. The list of rides and other entertainment on offer now included a Balkan Village with over a hundred natives; Mountain Slide, African Dip, Fun Grotto, Joy Wheel, Jolly Tubes, the smallest train in the World, Crystal Maze, Figure Eight and Aerial Flight. The Kursaal was advertised as 'Southend's Coney Island' following C.J. Morehouse's return from an American visit, and it appears that he brought back with him *The Whirlpools*, and a new Rifle Range.

Gypsies, soldiers and the zoo

At the outbreak of the First World War, advertisements appeared in the local press declaring that the Kursaal would remain open as usual. A group of Galitsian Gypsies from Austria[19] settled in the grounds in 1914 and, no doubt, operated some of the rides[20]. In November 1914 discussions took place regarding the use of the Kursaal buildings as the headquarters of the 14th and 15th battalions, Kings Royal Rifles. By the middle of December, a large detachment of Royal Engineers laid down concrete foundations for baths and latrines. Forty shower baths were ready by the beginning of March 1915. The main buildings were used as billets for the troops, while the grounds remained largely open as usual, with eleven acres of amusements. Two of the principal activities involving both visitors and soldiers were specially arranged

In 1914 a group of Galitsian (Austrian) Gypsies settled in the Kursaal grounds. They were on a tour of the south of England. Their success in the Kursaal is said to have persuaded C.J. Morehouse to continue with the amusements after the War. Photograph by courtesy of University of Liverpool.

boxing matches and shooting contests. The miniature rifle range was hired to the Third Border Regiment by the Southend Rifle Club. In the grounds were the very popular 'Knock the Kaiser's Head Off' and a reconstruction of the British trenches at Ypres, introduced in May 1915. Some of the incendiary bombs that had fallen on the town were also on display. At the front entrance of the Kursaal special accommodation was installed for a guard. The army vacated the Kursaal in June 1915, the troops being sent to Gallipoli[21].

The year 1916 saw the introduction of the Kursaal Zoo. Cages and dens for the animals were built on the site of the Tea Gardens; Mr Morehouse promised over 100 animals would be

Although the main entrance to the Kursaal was via the "vestibule" below George Sherrin's dome, there was also a separate entrance to the "Gardens". This may have been the original entrance to the Marine Park.

Apart from the "Menagerie" that was advertised at the opening of the Kursaal (and which was housed at the end of the Arcade) the first Kursaal zoo was introduced in 1916, with animals brought from Cobtree Zoo.

brought from Cobtree Zoo, run by Mr Tyrwhitt-Drake. The zoo opened on 10 June and among the animals on show were Sudanese sheep, a deer, llama, fighting ram, wallaby, ostriches, a lion and lioness, hyena, bears, panther, wolves and monkeys and eagles. Mr Crouch was the zoo attendant or keeper; Mr Whitehall was in charge of the Monkey House. In this year also, David de Forest Morehouse married Margaret Harper. In 1917 the Kaiser's effigy was hanged during the Military Night Ball in February, to the accompaniment of the band of the 29 Territorial Reserve Battalion.

So successful had been the fairground in the grounds during the war that C.J. Morehouse was persuaded to forget his ideas for building houses on the site and to expand the amusements.

Following the declaration of peace at the end of the First World War, 1919 began with a six hour-long Victory Ball at the Kursaal and David de Forest Morehouse returned home after serving as a Captain with the King's Royal Rifles. Southend United Football Club took up the Morehouse's offer to play their matches at the Kursaal, on the ground lately occupied by Southend Athletic.

Clifton Jay Morehouse died in 1920, leaving the Kursaal in the very capable hands of his son.

**A plan of the
Kursaal grounds
in 1920.**

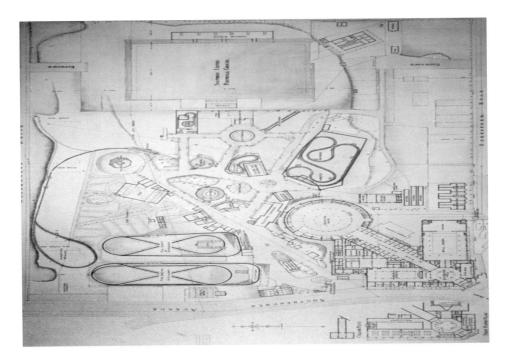

Compare this aerial photograph of the Kursaal (about 1920) with the plan. One of the most prominent of the
"rides" is the Aerial Flight. Notice also the plot of land to the right; this was to become the home of Southend
United Football Club until 1934.

The
David de Forest Morehouse years
(1921–1934)

Ricardo Sacco was the "fasting man" who, on several occasions, occupied a spot in the Kursaal, attempting to beat his own record for fasting. In 1927 he began his 50-day fast in a specially constructed glass fronted room in the Arcade.

The Spurs are united

David de Forest Morehouse was a director of Southend United Football Club and he extended the lease of the Kursaal ground to the club for a further three years. This enabled the Club to justify spending the money to make necessary improvements – and improvements were called for to accommodate Tottenham Hotspur who played Southend at the Kursaal in 1921. Southend United continued to play at the Kursaal ground until 1934.

The Water Chute and the railway that never stopped

New for the 1921 season were the Tumblers, Motor Roundabouts, a Dwarf Railway and the Whip, together with the Water Chute, brought directly from Earls Court, where it had operated from 1893 to 1914. This latter ride proved to be one of the most popular in the Kursaal gardens, and one of the most successful. It was one of the few rides, especially in later years, to have constant queues.

In June there was an announcement that the Kursaal was to stage a series of high class concerts, to be held fortnightly, and opening with Dame Clara Butt.

In July an inquest was held into the death of Mrs Ellen Clarinda Smith, who fell to her death from the Harton Scenic Railway, and in October the Joy Wheel was again destroyed by fire, taking less than half an hour to burn to the ground.

David de Forest Morehouse was a Director of Southend United Football Club – this is the 1925–6 season's team – and had extended the lease of the Kursaal ground to the Club. This enabled the Club to spend the money necessary to upgrade the ground in order to host the game with Tottenham Hotspur.

One of the most famous of all the attractions in the Kursaal was the Water Chute. It was introduced in 1921, having been brought directly from Earls Court. It was one of the few rides in the grounds for which there was always a queue.

A passenger's view of the waterchute. Although tame by the standards of the big rides of today, this was always guaranteed to thrill the audience, with the anticipation of a good soaking at the end!

There were several roller coasters in the Kursaal, from 1894 up to 1973. The Harton Scenic Railway of 1910 was one of the earliest and survived until the closure of the park in 1973.

C.J. Morehouse offered the Kursaal for the holding of the "Old People's Dinner", an annual charity event for residents aged about 70 years and over. The dinner had begun in the 1870s, but was transferred to the Kursaal, with catering by Garons.

Such disasters, however, did nothing to lessen the popularity of the Kursaal. In December the Southend and District Canine Society dog show was held and, in the following January 1922, the Old People's Dinner was organised. The first annual Old People's Dinner had been held in 1877, later being transferred to the Kursaal, coming under the patronage of the Morehouse family. Another annual charity event was the Children's Party for underprivileged children. This was sponsored by the Alexandra Yacht Club and the catering for both was provided by Garons (the dinners were funded from various sources, especially charity events). Each year the Kursaal staff were taken on their annual outing; in 1921 this was to Maidenhead, and in 1922 to Hampton Court.

In March 1922 the Rotary Industrial Exhibition was opened by the Lord Mayor of London. This was a trade exhibition featuring local industries and shops.

The new indoor bowling game of *Skeeball* was introduced in 1923 and other new attractions for this season included *Kelly's Cottage* and Marvellous Mirano, who performed various daring aerial acts from a specially constructed ride. Mirano's partner would sit in a torpedo-shaped carriage suspended from one arm of the structure (acting as a counterweight) while Mirano himself would perform trapeze acts on the high wire suspended from the other arm. He performed twice daily, at 4pm and 8pm. A music licence was obtained in the same year for Sunday performances in the Kursaal Kinema.

The major new attraction for 1923 was the *Never Stop Railway*. Opened for its trial run on August Bank Holiday, the ride consisted of a group of carriages which ran on a continuous track, arranged in two lines about six feet (almost two metres) apart; one was the 'up' line and

Mirano performed daring acts twice daily, at 4 pm and 8 pm and was a great attraction.

Alex Mirano or "The Marvellous Mirano" performed his high wire acrobatic act from 1923. His trapeze was counterbalanced by a torpedo-shaped chair in which his partner rode.

the other the 'down' line. The carriages ran continuously on this track, powered by a graduated 'screw' mechanism; this allowed the carriages to slow to a speed of about two miles per hour at the stations (thus allowing people to board and alight from the train), and speeding up to about 16 miles per hour (or more) between stations. Each carriage could accommodate eight people sitting and another four standing, and carrying capacity of the whole system was said to be 18,000 an hour. According to the advertisements in the local newspaper, the great novelties of the *Never Stop Railway* (installed by Never Stop Transit) were that it needed no brakes, no signals, no driver, no conductor, and causes no noise, no jerks, no crowding and no accidents.

Mr Morehouse was praised in the pages of the *Southend Standard* for his promotion of important and serious developments in practical science and well as the amusement of the masses. However, advertisements for the *Never Stop Railway* ceased after a couple of years, so we must assume that the venture was not the success it was hoped for.

Fully booked for winter

During the winter months, whilst the grounds were closed, the Kursaal buildings were fully occupied. There were exhibitions, demonstrations, hockey and skating matches, the Kinema, events in the Ballroom and billiards. There was a Girl Guides demonstration in February 1924, the Southend Rotary Industrial exhibition in October of the same year opened by Lord Elvedon and political meetings such as Stanley Baldwin's in October 1924 and the Southend Conservatives in December. The winter months, of course, provided the opportunity to repair and paint many of the rides and stalls. Some of the tenants would join other shows or fairgrounds (such as Olympia) to earn extra money, while many had to ensure that their takings from the summer season would last them all year until the following spring.

Slots of fun

One of the most successful of the enterprises in the Kursaal was the manufacture of amusement machines on the premises. In 1921 the company of Smith, Paine and Grant was established, which became the Essex Auto Manufacturing Company Limited in 1923. By the late 1920s they were making dozens of different slot machines, including *The Football Game* and *The Racer* (a greyhound racing game). All of the background scenes for the machines were painted by F. C. Seaton. The machines were supplied to many other seaside venues including Blackpool. Later, this same firm was making an automatic newspaper dispenser, which was exported to America.

Zulus, artificial ice and Sacco, the fasting man

In April 1925 we find advertisements for the Zulu Warriors and the Snake Pit. These 'warriors' and the occupants of the Native Village were (we are told) workers from the East India Docks, who would supplement their earnings by appearing at the Kursaal, dressed in grass skirts[22]. The Zulu village was managed by Gordon Stumcke, while his father, Frank, managed the Snake Pit. There may also have been an earlier snake pit introduced by Arsene Lecorgne[23].

One of the best known of the showmen in the 1920s and 1930s was Gordon Stumcke who, with his father, managed some of the most famous of the sideshows and acts. Among these was the Zulu Village, complete with grass-skirted "natives".

The Essex Automatic Manufacturing Company, based at the Kursaal, was one of the largest makers of amusement machines in the country. Here we see their stand at the British Industries Fair Exhibition, 1930.

The Zulu warriors at the Kursaal were, it has been claimed, workers from the East India Docks, who would earn a few extra shillings by dressing up in grass skirts for the crowds at the Kursaal.

In 1921 the company of Smith, Paine and Grant was established at the Kursaal, changing its name to the Essex Auto Manufacturing Co. Ltd. in 1923. By the late 1920s they were making dozens of different amusement machines, many of which were exported.

In July the newest attraction was opened: the Toboggan and artificial ice ride. The Toboggan, similar to one at Wembley, was 420 feet long, and had five separate runs, starting from a height of 55 feet, and gliding on artificial ice. The ride was constructed by Crystal Artificial Ice on behalf of Winter Sports Limited. Winter attractions at the Kursaal at this period included badminton (in the ballroom and arcade) and skating in the circular rink. In 1926 hockey matches were held for the Kursaal Challenge Cup.

The Autodrome was the new attraction for 1927 and the same year saw several events held in aid of the Victoria Hospital. These included a grand Bazaar, organised by the ladies of the Working Party of Southend Victoria Hospital, and a boxing tournament. Greyhound racing was also held for the first time this year at the Kursaal (on the football ground), but the most popular attraction of that year was undoubtedly the incredible fasting man, Ricardo Sacco. In a specially constructed glass case situated at the end of the Arcade, Sacco began his 50-day fast on 16 July. Throughout this time he remained permanently on view; his only sustenance being mineral water (supplied by Ledicotts and Green) and cigarettes, supplied by the local firm of A. L. Edwards. The only furniture in the 'room' was a bed, an easy chair, a table (at which Sacco would write) and a hand basin. Signed photographs of Sacco could be bought for 2d each.

Sacco's first meal at the end of his fast was an egg beaten up with milk, with a dash of brandy, followed by beef tea. It was reported that at eight o'clock on the evening (advertised

Jack Hayden and Caroline Welland, champion skaters, in the Kursaal grounds in 1925. Many years previously, the Circus ring had been converted to a roller skating rink, and was known as the Crystal Rink.

A view from the top of the old Water Chute, taken about 1930. In the middle is the Aerial Flight, dating from 1894. To the right is the "Ice Toboggan".

as the end of the fast) the Arcade was packed with at least a thousand people. A loud cheer rang out as Sacco took his first sip of egg and milk. Over the course of his fasting almost 80,000 people were said to have visited him[24].

Motorbikes, midgets and Eric the Whale

One of the most famous of all the attractions at the Kursaal was the *Wall of Death*. This was introduced in June 1929 and was advertised as America's greatest thriller, coming directly from Coney Island, New York. The riders of this early *Wall of Death* were Marjorie and Billy Ward and 'Cyclone' Jack Cody. The structure was built by Flaxmans of Southend for the Motor Silodrome (Pty) Limited of which Mr Moore was the business manager. The Silodrome was a cup-shaped structure, with vertical walls, the bicycle riders defying gravity by riding around the vertical wooden walls of the structure at speeds between 26 and 40 miles per hour (advertisements, of course, claimed speeds of up to 100 miles per hour!) The show had already toured Australasia, South Africa and the United States of America, before becoming one of the more permanent attractions at the Kursaal. The following year the Mayor of Southend was among the first to see Earl Ketring drive a car (an Austin Seven) in the *Wall of Death*. The car had been adapted for the purpose, by having a body made of aluminium (by Messrs Sunny Dawes of West Road, Prittlewell), and the silencer removed. The tyres were also pumped to a pressure of 60 pounds per square inch. The feat had first been performed by Ketring and his assistant Nadine in America and they had been practising all winter. By April 1930 Tommy Kelly had become manager of the *Wall of Death*.

Sideshows and other attractions advertised for 1930 included Rameses (an illusionist) in the Temple of Magic and the Palace of Mysteries; and there were special children's rides – Kidsport, Coasters and Juvenile Roundabouts. Other attractions for 1930 included the Midget Mansion, the home of Colonel and Mrs Cox 'themselves midgets without deformity of any kind'. The mansion was designed by Mr E. W. Miller and was brought to the Kursaal in sections from London where it had been manufactured. The building was Tudor in style, about half normal size, and two-storied. It was provided with a library containing about 300 books, including the complete works of Shakespeare, all, again, about half size. There was a drawing room, a music room (with midget piano), a kitchen, dining room and lounge. Visitors to the Kursaal were invited to go in, for a fee, of course.

In October of the same year the Mayor of Southend (Councillor H. W. Richardson) opened the Kursaal's indoor golf course. This was an 18-hole octagon course, situated in the Arcade. In November, a golf tournament was held.

The following year saw the introduction of yet more new rides, such as *Rodeo*, *The Toss*, and *Ghost Train*. The Kursaal billiard room was converted to an indoor bowling green, which was opened towards the end of the year, and an Indoor Bowling Club was formed. In November the School of Golf was officially opened, with free instruction in December in the use of the driver, mashie and iron.

1932 opened with an announcement of what was to prove to be one of the biggest, and most memorable, attractions ever staged at the Kursaal. A huge whale was to be brought to the site. The original announcement in the pages of the *Southend Standard* declared that the whale was 73 feet in length (other descriptions claimed 50 feet in length), weighed 65 tons, and was to be on view from Easter, forming part of the Empire Exhibition. Eric, probably a blue whale, and certainly one of the Rorqual whales, had been shown at Olympia and

The Wall of Death was introduced to the Kursaal in 1929. It was advertised as America's greatest thriller, and it is to be supposed that de Forest Morehouse saw the Wall at Coney Island. The earliest riders at the Kursaal were Marjorie and Billy Ward and Jack Cody.

Balham, and prior to that, had toured America. The Eric the Whale exhibition was in the hands of Captain E. le Beroque, who explained to journalists that the whale had been captured in January 1930 off the coast of California. Its blood was replaced by 60,000 gallons of formalin, and it was daily sprayed with paraffin. Eric continued on display, to the south of the Water Chute, throughout the summer of 1933. The whale was housed in a sort of Noah's Ark, at one end of which was the pay box, and to the side a gangway to the interior. A contemporary journalist reported:

The Kursaal had its own Ice Cream factory. So famous was it that they even had this postcard produced to advertise it.

One of the attractions that is best remembered by those who saw it was Eric the Whale. Eric had been on tour in America before crossing the Atlantic, appearing at Olympia and Balham. One of the things that people remember about him was the smell!

The first and most immediately noticeable thing was the smell – the memory of it has lingered through the years. It was a heady, blatant kind of smell, a mixture of formalin, paraffin and whale – ever such a lot of whale.

Despite these drawbacks, so popular was the display that couples would get married in Eric's mouth!

In February of that year the Southend Corporation Electricity Department exhibition was opened by the Mayor, Alderman R. Tweedy-Smith. The main features of the exhibition included Eric the Robot, who would answer your questions 'politely and accurately'. Eric had been invented by Mr Vincent Holden. If a question was asked of Eric that he could not answer, his reply was 'I don't know. Ask a policeman'. During the exhibition 3,000 visitors saw Eric, and 3,500 visited the magic light show. The purpose of the exhibition was to demonstrate the latest in electrical domestic appliances, many of which were displayed in an all-electric flat. Altogether, over 23,000 people visited the exhibition during its week-long opening.

Preparations for the new season were in full swing by April 1933. Advertisements announced an aquatic spectacle called *Neptune's Daughters*, a demonstration and exhibition about making 'talkies' in a real talkie film studio, and another robot, this time Marveille the Robot, billed as 'the most wonderful thing on Earth'.

Bostock's Wonder Zoo

Thriving during this period was the Kursaal Zoo. The central feature in the Easter of 1928 was the enclosure containing monkeys. Originally just a handful (from India and South

There had been several zoos at the Kursaal, beginning with the Menagerie of 1901, Drake's Zoo of 1916 and a later zoo comprising mainly monkeys and the Monkey Jungle, together with the "Cameo" Zoo, which was destroyed by fire. The most famous of all the zoos, however, was Bostock's Wonder Zoo, which opened in 1933.

America) the total number of monkeys was said to have reached 500. Later in the same year there appeared an advertisement for the Monkey Jungle, while a full list and description of the Zoo appeared in the summer. The animals included nine tigers, a bear and baby leopard (trained by M. Fernando of Paris), lion and lioness, puma, polar bears, hyena, tapir, peccary, llamas, pelicans, wombat, kangaroo, anteater, wallaby and Tasmanian devil.

The Cameo Zoo contained a number of small animals including a baby alligator, squirrels, an opossum and a civet cat. In May 1933 the Cameo Zoo was destroyed by the same fire that also destroyed the Joy Wheel. The civet cat was the only animal to survive the blaze. It escaped when the door of the enclosure was opened, hiding under the cage containing Tornado Smith's lioness, Briton (*see Chapter 5*).

Later that year, a new Zoo was introduced at the Kursaal by Frank Bostock. Advertisements declared this to be a Wonder Zoo with wild beasts, birds and reptiles. The nucleus of Frank Bostock's zoo was to be the lions and tigers, joined in April 1934 by Boyer, a Burmese elephant. At the entrance to the zoo was an artificial sandstone cliff face. The perimeter of the zoo was occupied by cages for the animals, including colombus monkeys, tigers, lions, bears, a wapiti, camel, racoons, badgers, wallabies, wolves, agoutis, llamas, bats, jackals, an emu, sea eagle and pelicans. Another feature was the peacocks that used to roam the grounds of the zoo.

Noah's Ark, Mont Blanc and Al Capone's Car

Rides and other amusements for the 1933 season included Noah's Ark, Petboats, Mountain Dipper, Back to Nature and Mont Blanc. Also advertised were a diving pool, a 30-stone man and a 200 figure working model of a coal mine. Near Eric the Whale was the new boating pool, on which the Petboats (about 20 in number) could be driven; the pool included islands and gates, being a small-scale simulation of a dockyard. Noah's Ride was a carousel, in which the horses had been replaced by a variety of animals. Mountain Dipper was a form of helter-skelter and another novelty for the season was the Devil's Glide.

The Mont Blanc ride was introduced in the 1930s by the Lecorgne family, and proved to be one of the favourites in the Kursaal Gardens.

The main attraction for the 1933 season was Al Capone's car. A huge advertising campaign ensured that thousands of people flocked to see the real gangster's car, which had been brought over from America for de Forest Morehouse.

Al Capone's car, green in colour, had been specially adapted for "Scarface" by the Cadillac Company. It had bullet-proof windows, extra thick body work, and a rear window that could be opened to allow one of the gangsters to fire at any chasing police.

The main attraction for the summer season was, however, Al Capone's car which De Forest Morehouse had purchased from Chicago. A press release was issued from the Kursaal giving details of the car. It was a V8 Cadillac, specially adapted for Al Capone by the Cadillac Company. The body of the car (which was painted green) was lined with steel armour plating and there were one-inch thick bulletproof glass windows. The car was said to be capable of speeds up to 110 miles per hour and to corner at very high speed. The car was also equipped with Chicago police broadcast sets and police siren to allow speedy getaways. The back window could be opened in an instant to allow one of occupants to fire his sub-machine gun, which was concealed in a violin case kept on the floor. The driver also had a sawn-off shot gun attached to the steering wheel. The car remained on show for the 1934 season also. Mr De Forest Morehouse rode in the car, dressed as a Chicago policeman, and with sirens sounding, along Marine Parade, much to the surprise of the local police force!

'One Bright Spot'

In March 1934 Southend United Football Club moved home to the Stadium ground. They had been at the Kursaal ground since 1919. The town's third Electrical Exhibition was held at the Kursaal in April 1934, this year featuring George Robot, a successor to Eric. The Exhibition opened shortly after the installation of a huge illuminated sign to the side of the main entrance. The sign featured two juggling clowns holding a circle of coloured lights, and underneath were the words 'One Bright Spot'. The illumination was designed and constructed by Mr E. (Ted) Johnson of the Kursaal staff under the supervision of the chief electrical engineer, A.E. Kent, and used over 1,000 lamps and almost two miles of wiring! Ted Johnson also designed and built many of the major set-piece illuminations for the seafront.

Kursaal characters of the inter-war years

Frederick William Houchin and Arsene Jules Lecorgne were among the earliest tenants of the Kursaal, both dating their presence in the fairground back to the earliest years of the twentieth century. Frederick Houchin had run away to join a circus when he was quite young and, before settling at the Kursaal, he had travelled all over the country with his shows. He introduced many of the amusements at the Kursaal of his day, including darts stalls and skittle tables and a rifle range, and sideshows called Big Bertha and Pan-la. Houchin himself was an illusionist and escapologist. Perhaps the two most memorable of his attractions were the Football Practice game and the bicycle ride. In the Football game the punter was invited to kick a football (attached to a long piece of rope) at a series of figures. Striking the head would knock the figure over and win a prize. Immediately after the First World War, Houchin painted the figures to represent the Kaiser, resulting in vastly increased trade. It is said that in one day £30 was taken on this stall, at one penny a go (when there were 240 pennies to pound!) The bicycle ride consisted of a number of bicycles, all joined together in a circle. The speed of the ride depended entirely on the pedal-power of the people on the bikes. The *Southend Standard* called Houchin 'the doyen of Kursaal showmen'. A true travelling showman until settling down at the Kursaal, he encouraged other showmen to come to Southend to join him at the fairground where he remained until his death in 1937. He lived in Beresford Mansions, which had been built for Kursaal employees.

Arsene Jules Lecorgne was born in France, and had lived in England since 1901. He, again, was a travelling showman, with exhibitions at Newcastle, Yarmouth, New Brighton, Colwyn Bay, Portsmouth, Cleethorpes and Southend's Kursaal; the latter from 1902. Among the many side shows that he introduced were Sweets aux Champagne, Dandies (a prize for knocking the hats off the dandies), the Allies Tumbling Tanks, Shooting Range, Hoop La and Coconut Shies. He also introduced the ride known as *Mont Blanc*. As with the Houchins, the

Lecorgne's Sweets Aux Champagne stall in the Marine Park about 1910. One of the earliest of the stalls in the park, the title betrays Arsene Lecorgne's French roots.

The Hoopla Rings was another of the early attractions introduced by Arsene Lecorgne in the opening years of the twentieth century.

whole Lecorgne family was involved in the entertainments at the Kursaal. His wife Sarah supported him on the sideshows, and his daughter Ida and son Fred were never far away. Another son, Louis, managed the Whoopee Express ride in later years. Ida married Jack French, a professional football player with Southend United, and who played on the Kursaal ground. Their daughter, Yvonne, in later years, managed a shellfish stall in the grounds. Barry Lecorgne, another grandchild of Arsene, remembers the spiel that attracted the crowds to wonder at Miss Okito – the lady of the knife – whose severed head appeared to rest on the blade of a knife; all done with mirrors, of course, and one of the many illusions for which the Kursaal showmen of the time were famous.

Coconut shies were one of the most popular of all the attractions, and were, like so many others, a feature of many fairgrounds, past and present, travelling and permanent.

The Dandies, also a Lecorgne show, featured a group of figures, male and female, taking a stroll in "St. James' Park." The male figures, the Dandies, were in their best attire, with top hats. To earn your prize you had to knock the hats off as the Dandies moved around on their turntable.

Shooting ranges were always the most popular of all the Kursaal side shows. One of the first was introduced by Arsene Lecorgne.

Other attractions for patrons during the First World War were Arsene Lecorgne's "The Allies Tumbling Tanks" side show.

Another of Gordon Stumcke's shows was Togo, the snake handler. There was also a snake pit, but the snakes were quite harmless.

We have already mentioned Gordon Stumcke and some of his side shows, such as his Zulu warriors in their Native Village. He also managed several other shows, including Togo the snake handler and a lady who could keep a gas lamp alight using just her breath; there was also *The Living Dead*, another lady who, with the clever use of flashes and mirrors, would seem to fade away until she became just a skeleton, only to come back to life again. And then there was his electric chair. Made of wood, covered in brass, a lady would be strapped in, and a brass helmet place over her head. An electric lamp passed over her chair would light up, to show that a current was being passed through the chair and its occupant. The audience was encouraged to touch the chair. Actually, of course, no electricity was involved until a member of the audience did touch the chair, and then a secret switch would be thrown for an instant to allow a small current to flow. Another aspect of his show, according to a visitor who saw him in the early 1930s, was the sale of cards covered in luminous paint, which would glow in the dark and cure headaches! Dick Harrow, the 'heaviest man in the world', was also managed by Gordon Stumcke. Dick had a chair specially made for him by Lingerin of Alexandra Street, Southend. Gordon Stumcke worked with his father in the Kursaal, and Gordon would often be seen outside the Kursaal, encouraging people to enter the buildings and fairground.

Other sideshows of this period include Professor Simpson and his photographic studio, Rochez and his performing monkeys, a freak menagerie (including, for example, Blossom the six-legged cow, and a three-legged horse), and *The Seven Wonders of the World*.

This period, between the two world wars, marked the heyday of Southend as the East-Enders' playground. One group of people who are particularly remembered by Kursaal staff of the period are the so-called Monday Ladies, or the Monday Mothers[25]. Of all ages, and many in their finest Union Jack bloomers and fancy hats, they came down to Southend on Mondays (as their title indicates) to avoid, so it is said, the rent man. Arriving by charabanc (a predecessor of the coach), they would first of all go to the nearest public house, and then, when suitably 'merry' enter the Kursaal, heading for their favourite

Dick Harrow, another of Gordon Stumcke's acts, was advertised as the heaviest man in the world. He was so large that a chair had to be specially built for him. Another of the Kursaal "freaks" of the day, Dick died at the early age of 38.

rides – the Whirpools, Kelly's Cottage, the Tubs and the Water Chute. On this last ride their typical amusement was to try and tip the boatman into the water. At other times they would be seen, and heard, walking in the grounds, arm in arm, singing at the top of their voices. Whatever the real reasons for their regular visits to Southend and the Kursaal, and these may have been far more complex than simply avoiding paying rent, this important social phenomenon of the Monday Ladies would repay further research.

In the 1930s and well into the post war era Southend, and the Kursaal in particular, was invaded by the Monday Mothers. These were groups of women from the East End of London, of all ages, who would come to Southend on Mondays (to avoid the rent man it was said) to have a jolly good time.

However raucous the Monday Ladies may have been, they were far less of a problem than the brewery outings. On four Saturdays each summer the breweries in the East End of London sent their employees on their annual outing to Southend. Each time this resulted in fights, oiled by the free beer supplied by the respective employers.

This section concludes with the death of David de Forest Morehouse, at the age of 51 years. He was born in America, and came to England with his family, first to Birmingham, and then to Southend. During his time as Managing Director of Kursaal (Southend) Estates Company Limited, David de Forest Morehouse visited virtually every other seaside town in the country to ensure that the Kursaal was supplied with the most up-to-date amusements available. He was regarded with affection by his staff and was generous to other organisations; for example he lent the Kursaal ballroom annually for the Old People's Dinner and for the Christmas Tea given by the Alexandra Yacht Club to children. From 1922 to 1934 he was Chairman of Southend United Football Club, and a member of Thorpe Hall Golf Club.

The Kursaal was now under new management.

FIVE

The Kursaal under Trustees

1935 to 1947

With the removal of the football ground in 1934, the way was open for the introduction of the Kursaal's largest ride, the Cyclone roller coaster. It came to Southend direct from the Brussels exhibition.

In safe hands

Following the death of David de Forest Morehouse, the management of the Kursaal was the responsibility of trustees under the leadership of the managing director, E.F. Williams, until Morehouse's two sons, and daughter should come of age.

The Cyclone

By March of 1935 mechanical excavators were at work preparing the old football ground for an extension to the amusement park. On part of this site was to be, among other rides, the *Whirlwind Racer*, and by April advertisements appeared for *Looping the Loop, Brooklands Racer* and special attractions for the Jubilee of the King George V and Queen. These included the Monkey Village (see how they work and play), and a new miniature railway for the children. A free attraction was Duncan, the famous Scottish escapologist, and, in the ballroom you could dance to the music of Harry Roy's *Lyricals*.

By May of the following year the Kursaal's famous *Cyclone* roller coaster had been installed, taking up the rest of the old football ground site. Designed by Charles Paige, the *Cyclone* had come to Southend from the Brussels Exhibition of 1935 and, with almost 3000ft of track and a height of 60ft, it was one of the biggest roller coasters in the country, similar to the large coasters that had been constructed at Blackpool Pleasure Beach in the early 1930s. The ride was, in fact, owned and operated by the Pleasure Beach Company both at Brussels and the Kursaal. Also in this year three other attractions were introduced: *Laff in the Dark*, a *Seaplane* ride and *Tumblebug*. Less than two months after the opening of the ride, eight

In the mid 1930s the Monkey Village was introduced by Harry Rochez. The monkeys were real enough, but their acts – playing music, operating a racing game, and many other "tricks" were controlled by a series of wires.

Hire wire acts, racing, playing the drums and ballooning, were just some of the "tricks" that Harry Rochez's monkeys would perform in his "Monkey Village."

Among the many famous bands and band leaders to appear at the Kursaal before the Second World War was Harry Roy and his "Lyricals."

people were hurt when two cars collided on the *Cyclone* and at the end of September 1937 a man was killed when he fell from the front seat of a car. Despite these accidents the ride continued to be one of the most popular in the Kursaal, surviving until the closure of the park.

The Tornado

It was in 1932 that George 'Tornado' Smith became the *Wall of Death* rider. He was joined the following year by his wife, Marjorie Dare. He was a great showman and owned a penny-farthing bicycle that he often rode about town, advertising the *Wall of Death*. Tornado Smith would perform various tricks on his Indian motorbike on the Wall including standing in the saddle, riding backwards and doing handstands on the handlebars. By 1934 he had introduced into the act a lioness, Briton, which at first sat on the petrol tank of the bike and sometimes on the crossbar. As the lioness grew larger, Smith made a sidecar for the animal. When not on the Wall, Tornado Smith could be seen walking Briton around the grounds and along the arcade, to the certain consternation of onlookers.

In December 1936 he was fined five pounds for speeding in his car. He paid the fine in farthings, halfpennies and pennies, having driven to court on his penny-farthing bicycle! Two years later Tornado decided that he wanted a change, and began to build a 12-ton Bermuda cutter in which he and his wife proposed to sail around the world. He reported that he was now not allowed to ride the *Wall of Death* on Sundays, and so decided to give up riding it altogether. However, in January of 1939 a fire destroyed his nearly finished boat, and with his wife

In 1932 George "Tornado" Smith became the principal Wall of Death rider. He soon began to make an impression with his daring riding feats, none stranger than when he rode with a lioness (Briton) on his bike.

he went to America. In August of the same year, however, he expressed his intention of returning to Southend.

Throughout the closed season, there were still held a number of events in the Kursaal buildings, such as exhibitions – the Table Tennis exhibition in March 1938, for example, and a Boys boxing tournament, talent competitions, and badminton competitions – and the Old People's Dinner every Christmas. In April 1938 the Southend, Westcliff and District Chamber of Trade announced that they would hold the Southend Home and Industry Exhibition at the Kursaal in October but this was later postponed until the spring of 1939. Also in April, the BBC announced that they would be broadcasting from a number of seaside resorts around the country, including Southend. The Kursaal would feature in the Southend broadcast, when listeners would be able to tune in and listen to 'the thrills of such rides as the Water Chute and the Giant Racer'.

Another war, the ballroom and plans for the zoo

Against the background of the gathering clouds of war, with ever increasing recruitment of Air Raid Precautions personnel in the town and announcements about air raid shelters, blackout and evacuation, events at the Kursaal continued as before. In February 1939 a Grand Police Ball was held, followed in May by the biennial Hospital Bazaar in aid of the Southend General Hospital. Throughout the second half of the year there were special guest appear-

Howard Baker was the resident band leader in the Kursaal ballroom from shortly before the Second World War until 1967. His "Old Time Band" played on Monday evenings, while modern dance music was played on Wednesdays and Saturdays.

HOWARD BAKER AND HIS BAND.
BEING TELEVISED AT THE KURSAAL, SOUTHEND-ON-SEA.

ances in the ballroom by famous conductors and their bands. These included Victor Sylvester, Billy Lawrence, Sydney Kyte and Oscar Rabin and his Romany Band. In August Reg Pursglove and his Broadcasting Band appeared, while at the Rivoli cinema they were screening *The Confessions of the Nazi Spy* starring Edward G. Robinson. Following the outbreak of war in September 1939, the local cinemas, including the Kursaal, remained open. Again, in the Ballroom there appeared Ambrose and his Orchestra (Vera Lynn was lead singer); Eddie Carroll came to the Kursaal to present his *Syncopation Piece* with his orchestra, and Billy Cotton led the Police Charity Ball in December.

Plans had been made to tackle the problem of the larger animals in Bostock's Zoo should hostilities break out. These plans were reinforced by public concern about the possibilities of the animals breaking out in the event of the enclosures being damaged. It was decided that the larger animals would have to be put down, while the smaller animals, including the monkeys, would remain for the present. Captain Sparrow, a local veterinary surgeon was employed to destroy the larger animals including Wallace, the full maned South African lion, Nero, the Abyssinian lion, and Sally the African lioness. Also destroyed were three wolves, two Russian bears, including Peter, the bear that Captain Varley (the lion tamer) used to wrestle, a Bengal tiger and three crocodiles.

The Kursaal remained open throughout the first half of 1940, with a continuing series of guest bands in the ballroom, including Cecil Black, Howard Baker and his Broadcasting orchestra, Miff Ferrie and his Jackdauz, Ray Scott, Harry Leader, Teddy Joyce and others. The Kursaal gardens opened at Easter but the outdoor amusements would have to close at 7.30pm, the indoor sections remaining open later. From the middle of May, Howard Baker and his orchestra were the resident band, with George Lester and the Novachord.

Lights out for the cinema

In early June schoolchildren from 19 towns in the south east were evacuated to places of safety (mainly Nottinghamshire and Derbyshire in the case of Southend schools), as, following the evacuations of allied troops from Dunkirk, the government imposed the East Coast Regulations. These, in effect, sealed off the south east of England from 'persons on pleasure trips'. Invasion was a real threat; Southend was now one of the towns in a 'restricted area' and, soon afterwards, a 'defence area' and visitors and holidaymakers had to leave. Southend was soon ringed by concrete barriers, pillboxes, barbed wire and gun emplacements. There were anti-tank barriers on all roads leading from the seafront[26]. The Kursaal was completely closed from the end of June, and taken over by the military authorities for war work. On 20 July, the cinema closed, never to re-open. The last film shown was *Bachelor Mother* starring Ginger Rogers and David Niven.

Uniforms, waterproofs and the NAAFI

During the Second World War the buildings were taken over for war work, and they and the park were closed to the public. For a short time soldiers from Dunkirk were housed in the Kursaal. The full details of the wartime work that took place in the Kursaal buildings, and the dates involved, are still imprecisely known. It appears that the cinema and other parts of the buildings were taken over by the Swallow Raincoat Factory. Mr Varani had been a partner in a tailoring business in Birmingham but left this to set up the Swallow Raincoat Company in

During the Second World War the Kursaal was closed to the public. The Water Chute basin was tarred to ensure it was watertight, and was to be used as a reserve water supply.

During the Second World War the Kursaal was taken over for war work. Here we see some of the ladies who worked in the Swallow Raincoat Factory established in the Cinema building.

the same city[27]. Here he was apparently making naval raincoats. There was a need for army and airforce uniforms and other protective wear, and he came to Southend to manage a branch of his factory in the Kursaal in about 1943[28]. Whether the factory was established in the Kursaal before that date is not known with any certainty. He and a Mr Smith supervised about 100 'girls'. A coach would transport the workers who lived in the more outlying parts of the area to the Kursaal, where they would start work at 8am, and finish at 6pm (or 6.30pm for the older, more experienced workers) Monday to Friday. Swallow Raincoats made principally raincoats for the NFS (National Fire Service) from 1941 (perhaps including the Southend factory) for both men and women officers, and WVS and Civil Nursing Reserve raincoats[29]. They also made RAF officers rainproof coats and camel fleece linings and waterproof trench coats. From October 1944 they were making demob raincoats[30].

The billiard room was used for cutting out the material; the Cinema hall was divided into four sections, and here the clothing was machined. Each machinist, or pair of machinists, was responsible for a particular part of the garment – making the sleeves, attaching the collars or lining, pockets, etc. Between each pair of machinists was a conveyor belt to transport the garment to the next machinists for the next stage in the process. At the back of the hall all the buttons were sewn on, by hand. The finished garments were then put on racks, and packed after being steam-pressed, in the Arcade. The Long Bar was converted to a canteen. The girls had strict instructions not to put anything in the pockets of the clothing; but, of course, they did, but whether any of the notes to 'our boys' ever got through, we do not know. It has been claimed (by one of the ladies who worked in the factory) that snow suits and other

Howard Baker's principal male vocalist was Johnny Thornton.

A new ride for the opening of the Kursaal after the war was the enormous Stratosphere Rocket ride. This photograph is dated 1945.

Arctic clothing was also made in the Kursaal, but this cannot be confirmed from the records[31].

Music while you work played in the old cinema hall, and the workers tried to guess which would be the final tune of the day, and on Friday afternoons the workers would sing along with the wireless. For many, working in the Swallow Raincoat Factory was far preferable to the Land Army and most (but by no means all) seem to have enjoyed their wartime work there. The Ballroom seems to have been taken over for war work, but it is not at all clear (further research might clarify this) exactly what it was used for. We do know that at least part of it was used for storage of military supplies including supplies for the NAAFI, the weight of which caused the floor to crack. Whether it was also used for the manufacture of military clothing, as well as the cinema (and other rooms on the other side of the entrance) remains uncertain[32].

The famous dome of the Kursaal was used as a vantage point for fire-watching and it seems that the dome was camouflaged during this period. The reflective surface of the dome would have been an obvious landmark to the enemy.

A fancy dress party in the famous Kursaal ballroom. These became a regular part of the New Year ball.

Restored and repaired

The Kursaal re-opened at Easter 1946 after a great deal of restoration and repair work. Advertisements appeared for attendants, cashiers, stilemen, fountains, cafés and licensed bars. The amusement park opened first at the end of April and the ballroom on 7 June, with a grand Charity Ball, the RAF Benevolent Fund Dance, with the RAF No 1 Dance Band. Howard Baker returned as the resident bandleader, with his Broadcasting Band, and with

Joyce Carlisle and Johnny Thornton as his vocalists. On 8 June there was a Victory Ball in the Ballroom, and in subsequent weeks there were talent competitions. Tornado Smith returned to Southend, as he promised, to continue as the *Wall of Death* rider and was almost immediately involved in an accident, coming off his motorcycle when riding the Wall. He was released from hospital after receiving treatment.

Saturday 7 September was declared *Hospital Day* when proceeds from entrance and takings from a number of rides was donated to the Southend General Hospital. There was also a Carnival Ball with fancy dress parade in the newly decorated Ballroom. The Kursaal showmen also dedicated a cot in the hospital in memory of their comrades who fell in the war. The *Hospital Day* raised a total of £1,650. A Grand Gala Ball with Billy Ternent and his full Radio and Recording Band in the early weeks of 1947 was also in aid of the hospital appeals fund.

The stars come out

As in the last few years before the war, a number of guest bandleaders had appeared with their bands at the Kursaal (often in aid of a charity), but Howard Baker remained as the regular leader. Throughout 1947 there appeared in the Kursaal Ballroom Harry Saville and his Broadcasting Band, Cecil Norman, Reg Pursglove, Ted Heath ('the Radio Favourite'), Harry Davidson, and Geraldo and his Orchestra. At a benefit ball at the end of August a number of well-known artists of stage and screen appeared, including Tommy Trinder, Greta Gynt and Joyce Greenwood, together with the bandleaders Victor Sylvester and Bob Bean.

In August 1947, it was announced by Clifton Jay Morehouse that he, his brother and sister hoped to be able to take over the running of the Kursaal, from the trustees the following month.

Six

C.J. Morehouse (the second)

1948–1973

Another full house in the Kursaal ballroom for a special concert performance.

The Kursaal in its heyday

There can be little argument that the immediate post-war years can be regarded as the Kursaal's heyday. The Amusement Park (the gardens) and the entertainment provided in the ballroom and arcade, together with the rest of the public rooms, were more popular than ever. Throughout the 1950s and into the early 1960s the Kursaal's car parks seemed to be always full of coaches. There were four car parks, holding a total of about 700 coaches (plus cars). At weekends coaches would stream into Southend for much of the day, a large number of them destined for the Kursaal. When the Kursaal was full to capacity, the coaches would park along the seafront.

Although precise visitor figures are not available, we can trace, through comments in the local press and from other contemporary accounts, the decline in visitor numbers that began in the mid-1960s. In 1969, for example, it was reported in the local press that there were about one quarter of the number of coach parties visiting the Kursaal compared with the immediate post-war years. The causes of this decline are not simple and, of course, Southend was not unique in seeing its traditional visitors seeking other destinations. We shall be returning to a discussion of these aspects later.

The immediate post-war period was one of repair and reconstruction for the Kursaal as five years or more of neglect and damage caused by war work in the buildings had to be repaired. One casualty was the Figure Eight coaster, which was demolished in 1947 to provide timber to repair the more popular Scenic Railway. The fairground and buildings were soon fully open again and by the 1948 season, 400 people were working in the Kursaal, many of them the same families as in the pre-war period. The floral decorations for the ballroom stage were grown in the Kursaal hothouses, and an ice-cream factory was producing 2,000 gallons a day; the Kursaal also had its own laundry and completely self-sufficient engineering and electrical works. In that year also, 3,000 visitors saw Goering's bullet-proof car, which

An aerial view of the Kursaal taken in the late 1940s. The late 1940s and 1950s were the heyday of the Kursaal, with the park at its greatest extent. The largest ride by far can be seen on the left of the photograph – the Cyclone roller coaster.

A rare shot of the Children's Racer ride, taken in 1948. *(Photograph courtesy of the National Fairground Archive)*

In 1949 it was proposed to convert the Pillar Hall (formerly the Cinema) into an indoor swimming pool. However, despite much support, the plans were not carried out.

was capable of speeds up to 108 miles per hour. The windows of the car were, it was said, scarred by bullets from British troops.

Major plans were proposed in 1949 for the conversion of the Pillar Hall into an indoor swimming pool. This was the former cinema building, which had been the home of the Swallow Raincoat factory in the war. The Kursaal management had suggested the conversion of the building some years earlier, and it was hoped to employ local labour in the work. It was also suggested that that the pool would be used by residents (rather than by trippers), for schools and water polo matches. On the ground floor would be two cafes, and hot and cold showers for the swimmers. The lighting was to be a special feature. However, the plans were not carried out.

1950 was a General Election year, and the proprietors of the Southend Standard installed a teleprinter at the Kursaal – in the arcade – with the results being announced over 'Radio Kursaal'. Over a thousand people gathered in the Arcade to listen to the results as they came in. In June the BBC's Richard Dimbleby, Brian Johnston and Barry Edgar were commentators at the first ever live broadcast from Southend, including the Kursaal, and thousands of Londoners stayed on at the Kursaal in the hope of being televised.

In 1951 the most famous of all the Southend Carnival floats was made in the grounds of the Kursaal by the staff. This was the Kursaal Flyer, which was a replica of the American locomotives of the 1860s. Six men were employed in its construction, which took just three weeks.

Radio Kursaal was the voice of the Kursaal; playing "There's No Business Like Show Business" to end the day, the Radio was also used to alert the police and security to any trouble in the grounds.

The Arcade was a favourite with the crowds who would be encouraged to try to win the many prizes that were on offer in the shooting ranges, darts stalls and many others.

The rifle range was one of the most popular of all the arcade stalls. Rifle ranges had been a feature of fair grounds from the later 19th century, when they had been set up on Pawley's and the other seafront greens. They still hold their attraction today.

Another of the favourite Arcade stalls was the Darts Stall. It is a typical side show of both travelling and more permanent fairs, and always extremely popular.

Another of the darts stalls in the Kursaal, probably about 1920. This was one of the favourite types of side shows with the visitors.

Brian Johnston interviewing some of the young visitors in the 1950s.

A keyless organ was mounted on a tractor over which the carriage was built, and the engine and tender were mounted on a 30 cwt. Austin Tipper. The Kursaal Flyer appeared in carnivals in many parts of the country, and a local pop group (the Kursaal Flyers) even named themselves after the carnival float. A smaller version, the Kursaal Cub was built later.

Several outside broadcasts were shot at the Kursaal. Brian Johnston was seen several times making broadcasts for BBC television; here we see the Jets featuring in one of the broadcasts.

The Kursaal Flyer, the most famous of all the Carnival floats. It was built by Kursaal employees in one of the car parks, making its inaugural run in 1951.

Bands and bandleaders

Howard Baker remained the resident bandleader at the Kursaal until his retirement in 1967. Every Monday evening there was Old Time Dancing to his Old Time Band and on Wednesdays and Saturdays, modern dances. Howard Baker was manager of many bands and was known as London's uncrowned gig king. In 1953 Charles Cratham, of BBC radio and television fame, became the new Master of Ceremonies at the Kursaal ballroom, replacing George Anderson, who resigned after 30 years. It was also in this year, in February, that the ballroom floor was completely submerged during the disastrous floods. Old Time dancing did continue as usual, but in a restricted area of the ballroom.

During this period a large number of other bands and bandleaders made guest appearances; these included Joe Loss and his Ambassador's Band (for example, at the Police Ball of November 1952). In April 1954 there was a Royal Command Variety Performance from the ballroom, with the bandleader billed as radio's greatest musical attraction, Stanley Black and his Orchestra. He and his music had featured in more than 30 radio programmes and 20 films. Johnny Dankworth and his Orchestra (with Cleo Lane) appeared in the later 1950s, and the Eric Delaney Band made regular appearances from 1956 to 1958. In 1956 the doors of the Kursaal had to be closed as Eric Delaney played to a completely full house. Ted Heath and his Orchestra (which was formed in 1945) appeared at the Kursaal from 1956 to 1959 and the Kirchin Band in 1956 and 1957, and Ken Mackintosh with his orchestra throughout the 1950s.

The later 1950s saw a gradual increase in the numbers of young people in the Kursaal ballroom, keen to hear, and dance to, the latest music. Howard Baker began to introduce modern skiffle and pop groups as his interval bands. Among these were the Del Rio Five. The jiving and jitterbugging of the period caused the Kursaal management problems and was not allowed in the ballroom. Being a sprung floor, the latest dance craze caused not only the mirror ball suspended from the ceiling to move alarmingly, but the whole building to vibrate!

In February 1953 the south and east coasts of England were devastated by floods. Canvey and other low-lying areas around south east Essex were some of the worst affected. Here we see Arnold Avenue and part of the Kursaal grounds the day after the floods.

Basil Kirchin made guest appearances with the Kirchin band in the Kursaal ballroom in 1956 and 1957.

In 1958 Jim Dale, presenter of BBC's *6.5 Special* television programme, piloted the show in a broadcast from the Kursaal, featuring The Mudlarks, Mona Baptiste, The Five Dallas Boys, Don Rennie, and Claudio Venturelli. Eric Delaney also appeared with his band, together with Tito Burns, the 6.5ers, the Kingpins, and Tony Osborne and his Brasshats. An audience of 500 local teenagers came in for dress rehearsals, and Frankie Howerd made a guest appearance.

In February of the following year the ballroom was again turned into a television studio, this time for the *Top Town* tournament, produced for the BBC by Barney Colehan. Southend won by 16 points to Portsmouth's nine. The show featured singing OAPs, the Nankevilles, Cockney barrow girl, Vera Dorian and fire-eater Douglas Chadwick.

Many bands and band leaders made guest appearances in the Kursaal ballroom, none more famous than Ken Mackintosh. He and his band appeared in the ballroom throughout the 1950s.

With the new dances and music of the 1950s, Howard Baker introduced modern groups to play during the intervals. One of the earliest was the Del Rio Five.

In June 1960 there was the Schools Music Festival (which became an annual event), followed in September of the following year by a brass band contest, organised by Southend United Football Club Supporters.

The newest dance craze – the Twist – which, together with the fashionable stiletto heels worn by ladies, combined to seriously damage the floor of the ballroom, the surface of which was breaking up. In March 1962, over £2,500 was spent on the installation of a new ballroom floor. This was made of stronger stuff – English oak from the Duke of Bedford's estate at Woburn Abbey.

A major problem for the Kursaal management was the new dance craze of jiving and jitterbugging. The jumping up and down had to be prohibited to prevent structural damage to the ballroom.

The new dance craze of the "twist," combined with stiletto heels had caused considerable damage to the ballroom floor. It had to be relayed in 1962, this time using oak from the Woburn Abbey estate.

From 1963 the ballroom hosted a series of popular music competitions for beat groups and rock groups. Among the groups appearing were Frankie and the Dream Weavers (from Rochford, with Frank Cornish), the Baronets (also Rochford), the Phantoms and The Zodiacs (Billericay), together with The Nomads and The Drifters. There were 70 groups competing for the title of the best all-Essex Rock Group, among these being The Senators, Dave and the Classics, and The Outriggers, who won the first round. The first prize was £50 and a recording session with Decca Record Ltd. The semi-finals were held in July. The finalists were Dave and the Strollers (from Hornchurch), Scrooge and the Misers (from Harold Hill) and The Differents from Brentwood. A double-decker bus transported the supporters of Dave and the Strollers from Basildon to the Kursaal for the finals in November 1964. The eventual winners, however, were Scrooge and the Misers.

Among the many groups appearing in the first of the "beat group" competitions held in the Ballroom, in 1963, was Frankie and the Dreamweavers, led by Frank Cornish.

The Zodiacs also appeared in one of the pop group competitions in the Kursaal Ballroom.

The following year the competition was repeated under the title *All-Essex New Sound* beat competition. The competing groups included The Topics, The Fenders, The Artics, The Dynamics, The Dolphins, The Pentad, The Corsairs, The Road Runners, The Spectres and Blues by Four. The Spectres, who got to the semi-finals, comprised five lads who had all attended FitzWimarc School in Rayleigh. In their heats they played two Beatles numbers (*It Won't be Long* and *Money*) and the Rolling Stones number *I Wanna Be Your Man*. The Chevrons won the semi-finals; this group was made up of Trevor Franks, Clifford Franks,

The group "Scrooge and the Misers" from Harold Hill won the 1963 beat and rock group competition, defeating Dave and the Strollers from Hornchurch and The Differents from Brentwood.

The Nomads also competed in the band competitions in the 1960s.

Blues By Four appeared in the 1964 "All Essex New Sound" beat competition in the Kursaal ballroom. They were competing with The Topics, The Fenders, The Dynamics and many other hopefuls.

Scoring was by a "Clapometer", and so the more supporters who could be attracted, the more chance that band had of winning. Several groups (or their fan clubs) hired buses to transport the fans to the Kursaal.

Waiting for the results of the Clapometer was always a tense time for both the bands and their supporters. Wining the competition, or even one of the heats, could lead to a recording contract.

Barry Ricker, Paul Tyler and Richard Saich. The Southend group, Les Ombres, were 50 points behind. Scoring was by a clapometer, the audiences of around 2,000 cheering their favourites on.

Many other groups appeared at the Kursaal during the 1960s, and a full list can be found in the pages of the *Southend Standard*. In 1964 a live version of Peter Aldersly's Radio Luxemburg *Pop Around* was broadcast from the Kursaal. A panel of judges picked 'hits' (and 'misses') from a selection of new and as-yet unreleased records. A very old and tested theme today, but in the 1960s this was very new and topical. The mid-1960s saw audiences in the

Another of the groups appearing in 1963 were The Baronets from Rochford.

Another of the many groups, hopeful of winning recording contracts, to appear in the 1960s in the Ballroom were the Cossacks.

ballroom of mixed ages, from teenagers upwards, reflecting the styles of music being played. On Wednesday and Saturday nights, Howard Baker and his big band sound catered mainly for the older generation, while the interval bands treated the youngsters to the contemporary pop music. One of these bands was the Ray King Trio (founded in 1957), playing for a fourteen month period in the Ballroom in the early 1960s. The trio comprised Ray Catling on lead guitar, Eddy Johnson on bass, and Doug Hobbs on rhythm guitar. They played swing jazz music, with a strict tempo, which attracted the attention of Howard Baker. The trio played at other venues in the town also, including Garons Banqueting Suite, and also played as the Haydn Combo and, later, the Zephyrs. Another interval band were the Baronets who played regularly in 1964 and 1965. It was from this period that the big band sound was having to give way to the huge demand for contemporary music, but while the two were on the same bill, it was quite normal for 2,000 people to be in the ballroom on these evenings listening to some of the finest bands and groups of the period and dancing on one of the finest dance floors in the country.

From the autumn of 1967, Frank Weir and his Music played in the ballroom. He had a six-month contract to play at the Kursaal following the departure of Howard Baker, whose contract was not renewed. In January 1968, following a series of auditions, Dennis Hayward was awarded the contract by C.J. Morehouse to take over as the resident band at the Kursaal. He had been the drummer in Howard Baker's band from 1954, and later became his principal arranger. After Howard Baker's departure, Dennis Hayward put together his own band and, when it was ascertained that Howard Baker's contract was not going to be renewed, he offered to take his place. From February (1968) he led his 14-piece band on Saturday nights, from 8-11.30pm in the ballroom and a nine-piece band on Wednesday nights, from 8-11pm in

One of the best known of all the interval bands to appear in the 1960s at the ballroom was the Ray King Trio, founded in 1957 by Ray Catling. Ray played lead guitar, the other members being Eddy Johnson and Doug Hobbs.

Dennis Hayward had been the drummer (and arranger) in Howard Baker's band, and he formed his own band to become the resident band leader in the Kursaal from 1968.

the Estuary Room. Soon, however, audiences for the big band sound and traditional dancing were becoming too small to make the ballroom venue viable and the Saturday night dances in the ballroom came to an end. Dennis Hayward played on Wednesday nights only, in the Estuary Room. Even the Wednesday evening band numbers were reduced, first to seven, and later to a trio. Dennis Hayward left the Kursaal in 1981. As we shall see, the ballroom in the 1970s became the venue for pop and rock concerts.

Fanny Craddock, bungalows and the circus

Dwarfs also featured in the Circus. These are the Seven Eduardinis from Spain, who appeared in the 1951 circus. There was seating for about 2,000 people in the "Big Top".

The Kursaal was the venue for a number of highly prestigious events in the post war period, attracted because of its spacious facilities. There were exhibitions, trade fairs, demonstrations and competitions, most of which were held in the ballroom. A *Meet South Africa* exhibition was held in September 1948 to promote friendly relations between the two countries. The following February saw the Southend Ideal Home and Trades Exhibition, featuring a television theatre. By the end of the exhibition a total of over 81,000 people had visited the Kursaal, to see the latest in household electrical appliances and other goods – clocks, stocking mending machine, percolators, kettles, lighting and television sets and a model railway display.

In June of the same year the Co-operative Wholesale Society (CWS) held an exhibition of 33 stands, and in October the Southend Chamber of Trade held their Home and Industries Exhibition. This was followed in November by a second Southend Ideal Home and Trades Exhibition, the centrepiece of which was an 'ideal' bungalow, fully decorated and furnished with an electrically equipped kitchen (said to be the housewife's dream). There were also daily fashion shows.

At the end of 1950 the skating rink was returned to its former use as a circus ring for the Kursaal's *Mammoth Xmas Circus*. Tiered seating for nearly 2,000 was installed, and the whole enterprise, with big top, was said to have cost £50,000. The acts were truly international (which caused some language difficulties), and included Princess Mariani and her lions from India, the Alfodi Troupe and the Flying Rexons (Sensational Aerialists) from Hungary, the Salobrals (a juggling act), and Count Roberto and his elephant from Spain, and other acts from France, America, Britain, Sweden and Belgium. C.J. Morehouse had travelled (it was said) 10,000 miles to see and book the acts. A second circus was staged in 1951. C.J. Morehouse again travelled across Europe, it was reported in the local press, seeing over 400 circus acts; he even tried some of the tricks himself – such as attempting to ride a mechanical horse – to immense applause. The acts in the 1951 circus included the seven Eduardinis (dwarfs from Spain), the Arozonas from Vienna, who juggled with razor-sharp knives, and the Four Daniels, clowns from South Africa.

In January 1952 the Ford Motor Company took over the Kursaal for a whole month to show their new Fordson Motor tractor. In the post war years, the Kursaal was frequently hired by Ford for launching its latest models. The Girl Guides and Scout Associations held their annual shows and rallies in the ballroom. There were also boxing, badminton and other sporting competitions. The film star Jack Warner was the guest of honour at the Press Ball held in 1952, to select and crown the winner of Miss Newsgirl, won that year by 18-year old

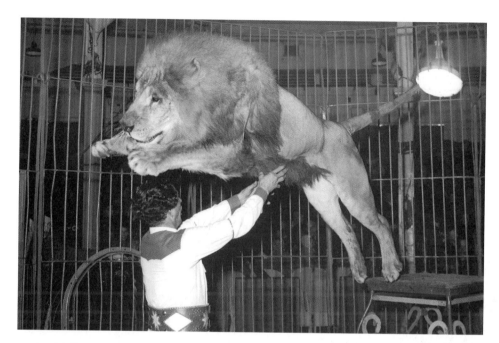

The Circus acts were truly international, with artists from Spain, Hungary, France, America, Austria, India and South Africa.

The Salobrals were one of the principal juggling acts appearing in the Mammoth Circus of 1950.

No Circus was complete without the Fire-eater.

Animals featured prominently in both the 1950 and 1951 circus; here we see the Zebras.

The Kursaal had its own Circus Band.

The guest of honour at the Press Ball competition to find "Miss Newsgirl" of 1954 was Donald Sinden.

The Kursaal had always been a venue for sporting events; at various times there had been indoor golf, cricket and now there was badminton, which took place in the Ballroom.

Wrestling was also featured, and here we see the Police wrestling competition.

Wearing full American Indian head dress, Billy Two Rivers prepares to take on another opponent. Bill Robinson looks on from outside the ring.

Another view of the Police wrestling competition.

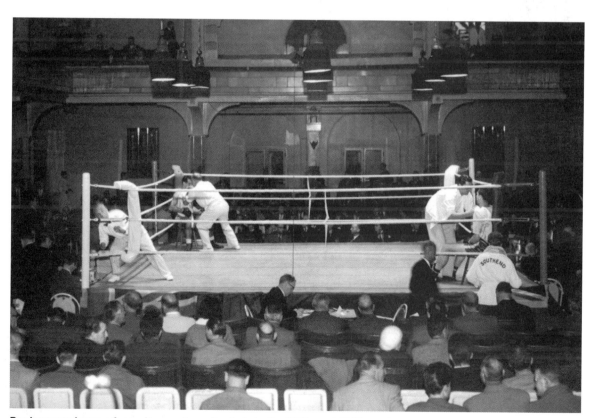

Boxing was always a favourite sport, particularly in the 1950s and 1960s, and was always well attended.

Angela Butlin. The guest of honour in the 1954 competition was Donald Sinden, the winner this time being presented with a holiday in Corsica.

Some of the most well-known television personalities appeared at the Kursaal in the 1950s, in particular the early television chefs. Both Eastern Electricity and North Thames Gas Board hired the ballroom for cookery demonstrations in which the chefs would use their latest equipment. In February 1954, for example, the Southend Standard reported that Philip Harben (the first television chef) appeared for Eastern Electricity:

> *From the moment he ran on to the Kursaal stage, vigorously stirring a saucepan, to the moment he ran off again, after showing housewives how to make a soufflé, pancakes, omlettes, crepe souzette and zabaglione, the Harben dynamo was never still.*

In 1955 there was *Kitchen Magic* at the Kursaal. Fanny (she was referred to as Phyllis in the newspaper reports) and Johnny Craddock starred in this promotion by North Thames Gas Board, which had planned the series of cookery demonstrations. The Craddocks appeared again in 1966 when Fanny presented three shows. The local press reported Fanny's 'machined-gunned hints' such as 'If you've got a queasy stomach you'll never make a good cook', and 'you shouldn't be able to smell anything cooking – smell is flavour escaping' and again, 'every man over 40 should have one glass of wine a day'. The audience applauded each dish, the report continued, as if it were a conjuring trick. Later in the same year the Southend Hotel and Catering Association staged a catering exhibition in conjunction with the National Cookery and Food Association. Lunch was cooked and served by full-time students of the Food Technology course at the College of Technology.

Among the other exhibitions held at the Kursaal during these years was the Police Road Safety exhibition of 1955. This was under the control of Inspector W. Devlin, and researched by Constable W.H. Jobson. The purpose of the exhibition was to illustrate road safety while telling the story of the growth of traffic from the eighteenth century to the mid-1950s.

North Thames Gas Board and Persil sponsored this event at the Kursaal, demonstrating to housewives the very latest in household appliances.

Exhibits included steam cars, boneshakers and other vintage motor cars. This was followed by the Daily Mail *Happy Housewives* exhibition in October of the same year.

Fashion shows were frequently held at the Kursaal. A fashion and food fair was held in November 1960, hosted by David Jacobs, and another fashion parade was held in 1962, opened by Cecily Courtneidge for Southend Priory Round Table and Ladies Circle. In February 1963 a fashion show, combined with a cookery demonstration, was presented by North Thames Gas Board's Persil Washing Bureau. This was specially devised for senior schoolgirls, illustrating the latest cookery methods on 'modern' gas appliances.

The Kursaal ballroom was the venue for many shows and exhibitions, among them fashion shows. For example, a fashion and food fair was held at the Kursaal in 1960, hosted by David Jacobs, and another fashion show was held in 1962.

The Kursaal saw many famous faces during its long history, with many scenes for films and television shows being shot on location. Among the many film stars to appear in the Kursaal was the young Kenneth Connor.

In the 1950s a private bar was created in one of the cellars of the Kursaal buildings. This was, apparently, to celebrate C.J. Morehouse's birthday, and the walls were painted by the resident painters. In the bar the walls were covered with many "French" scenes, some rather risqué for the time.

Another view of the cellar bar.

Other events included a live broadcast of the television quiz show *Whistle Stop*, presented by Macdonald Hobley, and included Beryl Schofield, later to become a councillor and Mayor of the Borough. There was also an Australian Trade Fair, to which small grocers from all over the country (in the days before supermarkets became the norm) were invited to see and sample Australian goods including tinned fruit, butter and cheese, rice and wine.

The Kursaal buildings had several bars, of course. Here we see the upstairs bar, with its famous "seahorse" mirror. That mirror is now housed at Southend Museum.

Perhaps the most famous of all the bars was the 1930s "Art Deco" or Long Bar, to the right of the entrance. It featured the wonderful sinuous bar.

A busy day for the Kursaal, with the famous Clown sign to the side. The special event was the Tradex Fair held in 1970.

A lady hits the wall

In 1951, eighteen-year-old Maureen Swift became the world's youngest proprietor-rider of a *Wall of Death*, when she succeeded Tornado Smith at the Kursaal. She had joined Tornado's team at the end of the 1948 season, and was trained to ride the Wall. She continued the following season but then branched out on her own at New Brighton. She returned to Southend, with her family, to take over running the *Wall of Death* when, apparently following a disagreement, Tornado moved his show round the corner to the Britannia Funfair. Maureen's mother made the costumes for her daughter, her father was in charge of admissions and her sister managed the catering.

There were then three riders on the Wall – Maureen Swift, Jack Campbell and Jack Brady – and when Jack Campbell crashed his bike in July 1951, Maureen and Jack Brady continued the show together. The following year Maureen appeared on the famous television programme *What's My Line?* In the mid-summer of that same year disaster struck as a serious fire damaged the bikes and the Wall. However, determined efforts were made, and Wall was rebuilt.

By 1954 Tornado Smith had returned to the Wall in the Kursaal. Early that year, in advance of the season he had placed an advertisement in the local press asking for girls to ride the *Wall of Death*. Nearly 20 applicants were received, and sixteen-year old Kathleen Leigh of Southend was hired and rode the Wall after just 10 lessons. In the same year Jack Brady, who was still riding the Wall, married his riding partner, Doreen Clark. The following year Juliet

Mitchell, 17, became Tornado Smith's latest protege. She was one of a hundred applicants who answered an advertisement in the *Southend Standard*. After her 10 lessons, she was riding 100 times a day.

In 1961 Tornado Smith was riding with Tich Taplin and Yvonne Stagg, performing three on a bike ride. In 1963 Tornado and the Wall featured in a film at the ABC cinema in Alexandra Street, Southend. Yvonne Stagg had been brought up in Sittingbourne in Kent but found life there far too restrictive for her personality. She wanted to have fun and excitement. At fifteen years old she went to London and found a job as a telephonist by day. In the evenings she worked on a rock stall at Battersea Fun Fair. It was there that she was first invited to ride a *Wall of Death*, and eventually joined the team there, touring the north of England with them. Later she joined other teams, touring Germany and Africa. On her return to Britain Yvonne went to ride for Tornado Smith at the Kursaal.

Another rider trained by Tornado Smith was Rick Abrey, whose stage-name for the Wall was Black Baron. He, Tornado and Yvonne Stagg performed the triple death race and other stunts, riding without hands and with feet on the handlebars of their BSA 500cc Star Twin machines.

Tornado Smith retired in 1965. In the previous year he had taught the young Laurie Gimbrett to ride the Wall. On his retirement, Tornado sold the Wall to Yvonne Stagg and Laurie Gimbrett continued to ride the wall with her, at weekends, until the grounds closed in 1973.

Fire was a constant threat in fairgrounds, as the majority of rides were constructed of wood. In September 1952, for example, the *Laff in the Dark*, a form of ghost train ride, was completely destroyed by a fire. The alarm had been raised by J. Martin, manager of the ride,

Tornado Smith was the most famous of all the Wall of Death riders. Here we see him revving his bike up on the rollers outside the Wall. This was done principally to attract custom.

which belonged to Parks Inventions and Devices Limited. The fire took the brigades from several sections 15 hours to extinguish, using water from the nearby Water Chute basin.

In that year there were over 20 rides and other amusements in the grounds, including the famous Cyclone Coaster, the Jet Planes, Caterpillar, River Caves, Ghost Train, Jolly Tubes (dating from at least 1920), Whoopee Express, Whirlwind Racer, Mont Blanc, Air Sport, Whirlpools, Gallopers, Bowl Slide, Brooklands Racer, Whip, the Water Chute (which had been in place since 1921), the Dive Bomber (a new ride), Toboggan and the Wall of Death, together with the 1910 Scenic Railway. The newest attraction was Noah's Ark, a structure 60 feet (about 18 m) by 40 feet (about 12 m) and 40 feet high, combining a house and cakewalk,

Yvonne Stagg joined the Wall of Death by 1961. She learnt to ride the Wall at Battersea Fun Fair, touring the north of England and, later, Germany and Africa. She then joined Tornado Smith at the Kursaal.

On his retirement in 1965, Tornado Smith sold the Wall of Death to Yvonne Stagg; shortly before that, he had also taught Laurie Gimbrett and Rick Abrey to ride the Wall.

sitting in a tank of water. This was modelled on the 1922 Noah's Ark at Blackpool Pleasure Beach (still operating to this day), which was itself modelled on the original 1919 Noah's Ark at Venice Pier, California. The Ark swayed up and down, had 450 feet (140 m) of passages, moving floors and wind jets. Out of the windows looked a monkey, giraffe, and elephant, while Father Noah peered out of one of the top windows. Also in 1953 began the construction of the Coronation Dome, a replica of the Dome of Discovery at the Festival of Britain. The Kursaal dome had been shipped from the Canadian Festival Exhibition. When completed, the Coronation Dome was used principally as a waiting room and traffic office for coach parties. It was opened by the film star, Joan Rice, in September 1954.

In 1952 the famous "Laff in the Dark" was completely destroyed by fire. Fire was a major problem, with so many rides being completely constructed of wood, and smoking being allowed everywhere.

The Gallopers were among the earliest of fairground rides, and have remained a firm favourite with visitors.

An interesting insight into the operation on one particular attraction, and the practical, rather than theoretical, relationship between a sideshow and its visiting public is provided by this account of the *Tip 'Em Out of Bed* side show, in 1955, reported in the local press. Maureen Sutton was the *Tip 'Em out of Bed* girl at the stall owned by David Fullerman. She earned £1 for a 10 _ hour day, which started at 1pm. Customers would buy seven wooden balls for a shilling (5p) and shy them at the target above the bed. So popular was this show that police sometimes had to control the crowds, some members of which would try to leap over the

The **Bowl Slide** was one of the most dominant of the Kursaal rides. It was rather like a helter-skelter, in which you sat on a mat to slide spiral fashion to the bottom. Here we see it in the 1930s.

The famous Carousel in the Kursaal Gardens. This was owned by the Morehouses, and was one of the most traditional of all fairground rides. *(Photograph courtesy of the National Fairground Archive)*

In 1953 the Kursaal made a special effort to decorate the entrance to celebrate the coronation of Queen Elizabeth II. Subsequently, a Coronation Dome was also erected in the grounds.

Whirpools in the Kursaal gardens, photographed in the 1950s.

Some of the Kursaal staff, about 1955. At the back (right) is Frank Wiles (plumber); in the front (centre) is Mrs. Beeton, manageress of the Canteen. Behind Mrs. Beeton are Jerry Frost and Bob Lawrence, and on the left, towards the back, Ernie White.

Airsport and Whirpool Rides in the Kursaal.

counter and hit the target with their hands, while others tried to hit the target with toffee apples and bottles. Americans were, apparently, the best shots, which Maureen put down to 'all that baseball'. By the side of the bed Maureen had just two items: chocolate and aspirins!

Laugh in the Dark was rebuilt by 1956, and was one of the many attractions for all those children who were given the day off school to celebrate Southend Borough's Golden Jubilee in April 1964. It was announced in the school assemblies that all schoolchildren would be allowed the day off to go to the Kursaal, where all the rides (for children only) would be one penny.

The Dive Bomber was a fairly short-lived ride in the Kursaal. It is known to have been in the grounds in the early 1950s, but had been removed before 1960.

The Caterpillar Ride was one of the firm favourites, particularly with the boys. When the canopy folded back, a gust of wind would inevitably blow the girls' skirts above their heads!

The famous "Tip Em Out of Bed" show. The resident lady would be "tipped" out of bed if you managed to hit the target with a ball. It was sometimes difficult to keep the young ladies, and the owners of this entertainment would often have to travel some distance to hire them.

All the fun of the fair. Another busy day at the Kursaal in the mid 1960s. This photograph was probably taken in 1964, during the Borough's Jubilee celebration.

In 1964, Southend celebrated its Golden Jubilee, and the Kursaal was one of the main venues for events and activities that year. Schoolchildren were given a day off.

All the rides were one penny (1d.) for schoolchildren; the place was packed by many of the Borough's schoolchildren, including the author.

A very good view of the northern part of the Kursaal gardens from the top of the Water Chute, late 1950s.

The old Water Chute, which had been in the Kursaal since 1921, was replaced in 1958. This photograph was taken in the late 1950s.

This Jellied Eels stall was run by Mrs. Chapman, a member of the Lecorgne family.

Steam Yachts, a much loved ride and, again, typical of the fairground rides of the time. (Photograph courtesy of the National Fairground Archive)

The Old People's Dinner had been an annual event at Christmas time in the Kursaal ballroom since the early years of the 20th century. Here we see one of the last to be held in the Kursaal, the 96th dinner.

In 1969 the Coronation Dome, erected to commemorate the coronation of Queen Elizabeth II, was home to the a Dolphinarium. The performing dolphins were Sinbad and Sally.

In 1958, the 1921 Water Chute was replaced by a more modern version. The new ride was mechanically-controlled and – unlike the original Water Chute – did not require a boatman to control the car. The ride resembled a roller coaster, with each car being hoisted up a chain-driven lift, before turning 180 degrees and plummeting down a straight drop into the water. The car then continued around the loop back to the station.

The vast majority of attractions depicted on the Kursaal plans of 1952 and 1956 were still in place in 1964 and, indeed, in 1973.

In 1969 the Coronation Dome was home to a dolphinarium. Sinbad and Sally were the performing dolphins, 'dancing, singing and playing bowls' in the 40-minute act. After leaving at the end of the season, the act went on a tour of Germany.

Seven

An era ends, another begins

1973–1998

The owners and tenants were asked to remove their rides and stalls, and the whole grounds presented, in 1973–4 a picture of forlorn desolation. A small area near to the Kursaal buildings was all that remained of the fairground.

Goodbye to all that

By 1970 the Kursaal fairground was still attracting visitors, but not in the vast numbers of the 1950s and even 1960s. In 1970 the Scenic Railway roller coaster – opened in 1910 – was taken out of service, and in 1971 the Water Chute was dismantled and moved to Ocean Beach Amusement Park at Rhyl (where it still operates to this day). In December 1972, after standing for three seasons without operating, a fire all but destroyed the Scenic Railway; its charred remains being demolished in early 1973. The decision was taken in 1973 to close the fairground and sell off, in the first phase, 20 acres of the ground for housing. In February 1973 the local press announced that the Kursaal could make way for a skyscraper plan. Plans had been presented first by Utopian Housing and later by Kursaal Estates Limited to the Borough for 750 flats in seven blocks of from 12 to 26 storeys, and 50 three-storey houses, together with pedestrian areas and a leisure complex. A spokesman for the Kursaal was reported as saying that

> There is a change in public taste in amusements. It could be that the public are moving away from the fairground atmosphere.

The opinion of many of the Councillors was that the Kursaal had become a 'tatty Victorian antiquated fairground'. In January 1974 the owners of the fairground rides had been given notice to quit, and requested to remove their rides at the earliest opportunity. It was in this year that the biggest permanent ride in the park, the Cyclone coaster – which had operated for 37 seasons – was demolished. Blackpool Pleasure Beach had been given only a few week's notice to remove the ride from the park. Outline planning permission was granted for the building of blocks of flats in the Kursaal gardens.

A five-acre area was retained at this stage and it was later planned to build here a leisure complex, possibly to include a hotel and banqueting suite. A small area of the park continued to function, however, with Dodgems, Wild Mouse, Jet Planes, Whoopee and Skid, and the rink and arcade remained open, as did the other Kursaal buildings. The Kursaal would operate in this much-reduced format for another ten years. Dennis Hayward continued playing – in the Estuary Suite – but now the Kursaal ballroom became the venue for a different kind of musical entertainment – rock and pop groups.

From 1972 a string of rock and pop groups, and individual artists appeared at the Kursaal. Some of these were already famous, some were to become well-known, while others were to remain in the shadows. The performers and artists included Rod Stewart, who appeared in 1973, Joe Walsh, an American pop star who began his British tour at the Kursaal, and Slade. Another American band, Steely Dan, appeared in May 1974. Among the other stars and groups appearing in this period were Chris Spedding, Thin Lizzie, Gong, Camel, Manfred Mann, The Stranglers, Hawkwind, Hot Chocolate, The Sensational Alex Harvey Band, Leo Sayer, Cockney Rebel, Deep Purple, Roy Gallagher, Black Oak Arkansas, UFO, AC/DC, Be-Bop Deluxe, and the Kursaal Flyers (who seem to have appeared only once at the Kursaal itself – their principal venue was the Blue Boar public house). Black Sabbath also appeared, as did David Essex, The Pretty Things, the Canvey group Dr. Feelgood, and another Southend group, Procol Harum. The 1975 Dr. Feelgood concert at the Kursaal was recorded, some of the tracks being included in their No 1 selling album *Stupidity*. The Sex Pistols appeared once, as part of their first British tour, in 1976. Status Quo, who had appeared at the Kursaal in 1972 and 1974, recorded their live concert at the Kursaal in 1975, the tracks *Roll Over*

In 1973 the decision was taken to close the Kursaal grounds. Visitor figures had been declining since the mid 1960s, as holidays to new and further destinations became available.

Barry Lecorgne, photographed in the Arcade, or "main drag" of the Kursaal. His family had been in the Kursaal since the early 20th century. The Arcade was the main route from the entrance leading to the gardens.

Inside the Kursaal's Casino, about 1970.

Lay Down and *Junior's Waiting* being released on an E.P. in May of that year. The concert was a complete sell-out, with a capacity audience of over 2,000. Other groups also played at the Kursaal, and for a full list the reader is referred to the archive held by Southend Museums Service[33].

In 1977 Kursaal Estates applied for planning permission to change the use of the Ballroom to a warehouse, with retail outlets. Although permission was refused, the ballroom was never

As the buildings were being run down, in the 1980s, the ballroom had ceased to function as a dance venue for some years. From the late 1970s the ballroom had been given over to pop concerts. One of the many famous bands to appear there was Dr. Feelgood.

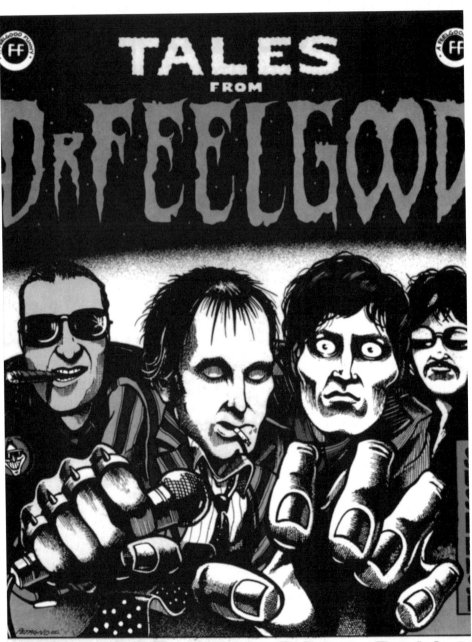

again a major venue for rock concerts. It is important to recognise that at this time, the mid to late 1970s, there were a large number of competing venues in Southend and beyond, particularly Basildon. Principal among these other venues were the Blue Boar in Victoria Avenue, Southend, where the Kursaal Flyers were originally based; Shrimpers, at Southend United Football Ground, also in Victoria Avenue; and Zero 6 and Tots in Southend.

The principal promoter of rock music at the Kursaal in the early to mid 1970s was local businessman John Paul. When the Kursaal ballroom was no longer available, he began, in January 1978 to put on weekly concerts at the recently opened Shrimpers.

The Arcade and other Kursaal buildings were closed in 1986, including the Kursaal radio station, which had been such a feature of the life of the fairground.

Closure and re-development

In 1977 planning permission had been granted for private housing development over the larger part of the Kursaal gardens or fairground. In 1986 the remaining 3.7 acres had received planning permission for further housing. Hey and Croft planned to build 180 more flats in two and five storey blocks. The Kursaal buildings continued in use until this date. There were still banqueting facilities, snooker rooms and the ballroom (presumably rather dilapidated by now) and Estuary Suite. In September 1985 a Nostalgia Night was held at the Kursaal, and in June 1986 the staff served the last meal at the Kursaal, in the Estuary Room, to the Knights of St. Columba. Shortly after this event, Kursaal Estates (with Kursaal Leisure, the casino) went into voluntary liquidation, the company being wound up in September 1986 with assets totalling over £1.3 million. The directors at that time were Clifton Jay Morehouse, C.J. Warry, and John Crowley[34].

The Kursaal was bought by the seafront entrepreneur, Peter Ketteley, who already owned a large amusement centre on the Golden Mile. He had plans to build a skating rink in the Ballroom, which would be the home of a newly formed Southend hockey team. However, no progress was made with these plans, and in early 1987 the Brent Walker Group was in negotiation to purchase the Kursaal buildings. They bought the Kursaal, and had plans for the installation of a multi-million pound development including the largest water theme park in Britain. Their proposals included converting the ballroom structure into a wave pool with cave retreat, waterfall and fun pool together with a flume pool and desert island. There was to be a newly built arcade leading to coffee shops and seating areas. The Estuary room would be converted to a Victorian street scene with seaside bar and rocket ride (a lift) and shop units. On the first floor level there were to be coconut shies and other side shows. These proposals were amended later to include a flight simulator with passport control and costume hire facility. Some of the buildings were demolished, including the Arcade, and the ballroom floor was removed, to make way for the water theme park. But as with the previous scheme, the plans did not come to fruition; the Kursaal was left in a state of dilapidation, and the Brent Walker empire collapsed at the end of 1991.

After 1986, for many years, the Kursaal buildings stood empty. It did not take long for the building to fall into disrepair.

The Kursaal buildings were placed on the Council's historic buildings list, and in April 1994 the dome and remaining structure were protected by the Grade II listed status by English Heritage. A full photographic survey was also made. The *Standard Recorder* newspaper set up a 'Find a Purpose for the Kursaal' campaign. In September 1994 plans of the Council to purchase the Kursaal buildings were approved, and a price was agreed with Brent Walker and the freehold of the property transferred to the Council. Inspections of the build-

The damage done to the buildings by neglect was such that much of the original structure had to be demolished.

The floor of the Ballroom had been removed (during the time that Brent Walker had the Kursaal) and the building was then just a shell.

In 1994 the Kursaal buildings were protected by a Grade II listing, and the following year the lease of the Kursaal was sold to the Rowallan Group for redevelopment into the leisure complex. This opened in 1998.

ings were undertaken, and by this time parts of the buildings were unsafe. Roofs were leaking and floors were collapsing, but the dome was in a state of surprisingly good repair. A considerable amount of water had leaked into the buildings, causing great damage to much of the interior, especially the first floor, and many original features and quantities of documentary material were lost.

A total of seven bids were lodged with the Council, and in 1995 an agreement was made to lease the Kursaal site to the Romford-based Rowallan Group for the development of a multi-million pound amusement, leisure and conference centre. After months of preparation and revision, plans were lodged with the Council in December 1995, and passed in the following January for a ten pin bowling alley, a skating rink, restaurant, health and fitness centre, banqueting and conference facilities, and a family fun and shopping complex. The plans were prepared by John Breley Design Associates and the developer, the Rowallan Group, and included an extension to the existing Kursaal buildings, but this latter aspect was heavily criticised by conservation groups. The Southend Society, for example, dubbed the design for the extension 'Fortress Kursaal' and said that it was entirely inappropriate. The problems were overcome and a lease agreement was signed, for a period of 199 years. Work began in February 1997, the contractors being Bowmer and Kirkland.

Hello to all this!

In February 1998 the building was handed over to the firm of Dean and Bowes for fitting out and in March 1998 the first phase of the restored Kursaal was opened to a specially invited audience. Following many requests to Alan Stack, Chairman of the Rowallan Group, he decided to have a special heritage opening to show the newly restored dome (apparently, 9 skip-loads of pigeon droppings were removed from the dome!) and vestibule, with its ornate plasterwork and stained glass. The event was a great success, and this part of the building then remained open for public inspection and over 6,000 people visited the Kursaal between March and May.

In May 1998, following massive restoration and rebuilding work costing £15 million, the restored Kursaal buildings were fully opened. The official opening took place on the evening of 14 May. With Second World War searchlights illuminating the Kursaal and skies, a carnival-like procession made its way from the foot of Pier Hill to the Kursaal. In the procession was the band of the Coldstream Guards, Warren Mitchell, the Beverley Sisters, Southend Sapphires Majorettes, TV stars Michaela Strachan and Matthew Kelly, Southend Mayor, Nora Goodman, and the MPs Teddy Taylor (Southend East and Rochford), David Amess (Southend West) and Alan Hurst (Braintree). Many 'stars' of the old Kursaal days were invited, and Ray Catling (of the Ray King Trio) led Crazy Rhythm in providing the evening's musical entertainment, together with the Brothers Grim R & B soul revival band and Southend guitarist Robert Tym. The Kursaal was opened to a massive firework show, including a 16 inch mortar, the largest firework allowed.

Many past Kursaal workers were invited, together with people who had fond memories of the Kursaal in its heyday. They could see the Café Kursaal on the first floor, with the Bourbon St. Restaurant; the Kursaal Bowl with its 30 ten-pin bowling lanes, American pool tables and hi-tech arcade games.

Crazy Rhythm, with Ray Catling, played at the gala opening, in front of a specially invited audience, including television stars, members of Parliament, many ex-Kursaal employees and others who once danced or played in the ballroom.

Whatever people think of the 'new' Kursaal, the important fact to remember is that the building has been saved for the town. And not only for the town, for the Kursaal played a significant part in the lives of so many people, both residents and visitors. The Kursaal was, and remains, a vitally important part in the history of Southend and also in the history of the leisure industry of this country.

The Rowallan Group had spent many millions of pounds in the redevelopment of the building, hoping to recreate some of the atmosphere of the old Kursaal in its heyday.

The Kursaal buildings live again. Of course, the Kursaal Gardens, the fairground, can never be recreated, but at least the buildings live on for another generation.

Select Bibliography

Details of primary sources used will be found in the endnotes. Details of references to the various newspaper articles quoted and used in this book are retained in the author's archive.

Abrey, Richard *Up the Wall in Keddies Review* Christmas 1969

Birch, Will *No Sleep 'Till Canvey Island The Great Pub Rock Revolution* Virgin, 2000

Keeling, C.H. *Where the Lion Trod* Clam Publications, 1984

Leigh, Imogen Wedd *Milner White and Partners* in *Landscape Design, pp 9-13*, August 1985

Pearson, Lynn *The People's Palaces: Britain's Seaside Pleasure Buildings, 1870–1914* Barracuda Books, 1991

Preedy, Robert *Roller Coasters: Their Amazing History* R.E. Preedy, 1992

Preedy, Robert *Roller Coasters: Shake, Rattle and Roll* R.E. Preedy, 1996

Walton, John K. *The British Seaside: Holidays and resorts in the twentieth century* Manchester University Press, 2000

Footnotes

1. The company registration numbers for these enterprises can be found in the Public Record Office.

2. I am grateful to Chris Izod for this information.

3. Extracts from terriers of the manor of Prittlewell Priory and other records, Essex Record Office, (ERO) D/DGS M174.

4. Southend Local Board Minutes, 5 July 5 1887, p352. ERO D/HS 5.

5. Southend Borough Council Minutes, Law and Parliamentary Committee, 28 March 1900.

6. Southend Local Board Minutes, March 1888, ERO D/HS 6.

7. Plan submitted to the Local Board, E.R.O. D/BC 1/4/11/695,696.

8. *Landscape Design*, Vol 156, (1985), p11.

9. ERO D/BC 1/4/12/212, 226, 247.

10. Public Record Office (PRO), BT31/6337/44784 and 6064/42917.

11. ERO D/BC 1/4/12/plan no. 1359; a letter accompanying the plan is dated 29 December 1896.

12. PRO BT31/7711/55090.

13. PRO BT 31/7711/55090, Articles of Association.

14. Sherrin was a very well-known architect, whose other works include Spitalfields Market in London, St Mary's Church, Eldon St. in Moorfields and Kensington High Street station. See A. Stuart Gray, *Edwardian Architecture, A Biographical Dictionary*, Duckworth, 1985.

15. ERO D/BC 1/4/12/1400.

16. *The Representative Journal of Aquatics*, 1 May 1897, pp10-11. I am grateful to Bob Bradley of the Margate Local History Museum for this and other references relating to the Margate Kursaal.

17. The East Kent Times, April 1905.

18. The Joy Wheel comprised a large circular platform (the wheel) which spun on a central pivot, and a padded area outside. The idea was to try to stay on the wheel as long as possible, as the wheel turned faster and faster.

19. Information from University of Liverpool special collections.

20. The Gypsies may have been invited by Mr. Morehouse. Information from C.J. Morehouse.

21. Information supplied by Major A.S. Hill.

22. Information from Mr. Joe Stumcke.

23. Information from Barry Lecorgne.

24. For reports on Sacco, see Southend Standard, 14 July; 21 July, p7; 8 September, p9. All 1927.

25. Bram Stevens remembered the Monday Mothers, whose favourite ride he described as the revolving tubs, in the days of De Forest Morehouse. The Monday Ladies continued to visit after the Second World War also, and are remembered by many policemen who had to try to control them in the 1950s.

26. I am grateful to Fred Nash for this information.

27. Swallow Raincoats Limited may have been part of (or an offshoot from) Swallow Manufacturing Company, Waterproof clothing manufacturers, of Birmingham, which

was established in 1921. (Information from Birmingham Libraries). Swallow Raincoats
    Ltd was established between 1930 and 1937.

[28] Swallow Raincoats Ltd, company no. 268965.

[29] The Ministry of Supply was established in 1939; they made contracts with manufacturers
    for the supply of all the necessary goods for the war effort. The manufacture of so-called
    Arctic Clothing, for use in Norway, began in October 1941. PRO. WO/32/9942.

[30] War Office and Ministry of Supply records, PRO SUPP/4/115.

[31] The Ministry of Supply's contractors for Arctic clothing does not include Swallow
    Raincoats. PRO SUPP/4/127. Swallow Raincoats do not appear among the War
    Department's index of 'Vital Factories' and so it may not be possible to ascertain further
    details of any other war-time products made in the Kursaal. PRO AVIA/12/71.

[32] I am grateful to Mrs June Lemaire, Mrs Jean White (daughter of Mr Varani), and many
    other ladies who worked in the factory for this information.

[33] I am grateful to David Oxley for much of this information.

[34] Information supplied by Companies House.